LeadG2
Getting Prospects
To Raise Their
Hands

Matt Sunshine

For my wife and daughters, who challenge and inspire me to think and grow professionally.

Contents

1. The New Sales Reality

"Today I will do what others won't, so tomorrow I can accomplish what others can't."

–Jerry Rice

Gone Fishing

If you're in business you know there are plenty of fish in the sea, but they're a whole lot smarter than they used to be. So how do you cast your net? How do you identify your best prospects, not just any fish, but "keepers"? Imagine being a commercial fisherman and as you're out on your boat, burning fuel and chasing these coveted keepers all over the ocean, you look over at another boat and see that its motors are idling and its crew is busy doing something different. The other crew is throwing bait and chum into the water, attracting lots of fish. You notice that your crew looks just as busy as the other crew— running around your boat, bumping into each other, finding perches and angles to scan the horizon, looking for fish and finding few. You watch the other boat. Not only is it burning less gas, it's also attracting the kinds of fish that you're looking for—those prized, tasty ones for which the specific markets and restaurants that you service will pay premium prices.

You're taking it all in, and it makes sense: by throwing desirable content into the water, the fish that you're looking for will come to you. Now if you're a commercial fisherman, you're looking at a mother lode—a full boat, one very happy crew, and a smooth sail home. If you're a decision maker at your company concerned with lead-generation initiatives—a Marketing Director, Director of Sales or Sales Manager, or an Owner—you're looking at the answer to a question that I know keeps you awake at night. What I've just illustrated with my little fishing analogy is applicable to your business and the very essence of inbound marketing. The more skilled you are at putting the right bait out there, the right way, the more likely that you will attract the best prospects—those that need you the most, and to whom you can be of most value.

Out With The Old, In With The New

"How do you identify prospects searching for information related to your product or service and then turn those leads into sales?" It's a serious question, one causing an unfair share of hair loss and sleepless nights. Many of you, nostalgic perhaps, are stuck in the good old days of predictable revenues (back when the fish were mostly uninformed and just didn't know any better). Following the time-honored practice of building a sales team, identifying your ideal customer profile or persona, working out the right compensation plan, and then letting your salespeople go out and do their "thing." You keep trying to do things this way to drive revenue. The bad news is those days are pretty much gone forever. The good news is there's an easy way to pivot. I'm going to share a we-can-do-it story about a company that did just that, more than 30 years ago, and has since dedicated itself to providing a remedy for that unfair share of hair loss and those sleepless nights. But before I get into my story, let me mention something about buying.

Think about how you buy things these days. How much of it is a result of an interaction with a salesperson? How much of your buying decision was already made before you ever spoke to a salesperson? Like you, your spouse, your peers, and your kids, *your customers* are buying in the same way. You don't need to write for the Wall Street Journal to know the marketplace has changed and, while most of the old norms are gone, some things remain. We still need salespeople. We just need a better way to optimize their talents so that we can maximize our revenues. First and foremost, we need to include ourselves in the prospect's buying process earlier. It comes down to working smarter and better intelligence-gathering—think of it as military intel, without all the drones. Returning to my fishing analogy, it means saving on fuel and letting the fish come to you. That's where LeadG2 comes in.

LeadG2 specializes in the advancement of lead-generation strategies for businesses looking to increase lead flow, gain lead intelligence, and improve conversion rates. We are developing inbound marketing tactics to help businesses drive sales and get results.

We focus on using target persona research and superior lead intelligence to develop the best content strategy for you to attract new prospects, nurture and convert leads, retain customers, and develop thoughtful leadership. LeadG2 is part of a sales performance company whose mission is to use inbound marketing strategies to effectively turn leads into new business.

Unlike many in the field, we are developing new ways of thinking and taking them from ideation to execution. Beyond just making pretty websites or writing clever copy, we are driven by performance. That doesn't mean handing off leads to clients and wishing them the best. It means providing customized training to help develop a true sales and marketing alignment that will take a company's lead generation program to the next level, to where it really matters most—the bottom line. Another point of differentiation and, quite possibly, the one we take the most pride in, is that LeadG2 does not just teach, we *do*. We practice what we preach and, as you'll see in the following section, it's all in the numbers.

Nothing Breeds Success Like A Success Story

For almost 20 years I've been teaching and talking about lead generation and how to grow sales, and if I know one thing it's that nothing rallies the troops like a good success story. One particular company that I often point to was started over thirty years ago as a one-man sales, training, and management-consulting firm. Targeting local broadcast and media companies, helping them generate ad sales, teaching sales process, and improving sales team performance, this one-man show grew and grew into the forty-person operation that it is today. That was no small feat yet hardly the measure of its success. For the purposes of this book, what's so successful about this company is its "stickiness." Over the course of its being in business, this company maintains a 93% customer retention rate. Its client turnover rate is no less impressive, with their clients on average sticking with them for over seven years. When it comes to customer retention, these guys are like superglue.

Further distinguishing itself from the competition, this company prides itself on the fact that all of their client-facing personnel were former sales managers in the field. They didn't just "talk the talk," they'd done it, they'd lived it—they'd "walked the walk."

About three years ago, this company decided that it needed to grow. To do so, it would need to expand beyond its core media vertical that had been its trusty bread and butter for almost the last 30 years. Convinced that their sales consulting and management training could and would apply to business-to-business (B2B) enterprises in other industries, they developed a targeting strategy for new clients with the following criteria:

- They needed to be a B2B enterprise
- They needed to sell to sell again, in other words, customer acquisition was more important than simply making a transaction
- They needed to provide a somewhat customizable solution
    - They didn't want to provide one solution to every client, but wanted to customize a product to fit each client's specific needs—just as the furniture company can customize dressers and tables to fit their customers' needs without having to custom-make every piece of furniture

With this three-criteria initiative they were all set to bring in a host of new clients, but one question quickly reared its little head: "How Do We Do It?"

What became immediately apparent was rather ironic for sales consultants and a sales training organization. They did not have any salespeople. Having retained 93% of their customers and keeping clients on average for over seven years, they never needed any. The way it had always worked was when a manager (customer) who worked in one division was moved to another, he or she would simply call the company and ask, "can you work with me over here now?" It was that easy and it had always been enough for solid earnings, but no longer. The company needed to go out and explore beyond its comfort zone and it was going to take more than just a well-thought-out initiative, it was going to take manpower.

Before I continue with my success story, I must disclose that this company was (and still is) The Center for Sales Strategy, and that "manpower" I mentioned was going to be none other than *me*. I had been a group Director of Sales who prided himself on innovative thinking. Raising my hand that day at the meeting, I was taking on the responsibility of tracking down this initiative and figuring out how exactly we were going to market.

Well, my colleagues sure dodged a bullet and, breathing a sigh of relief, all eyes were now on me. Diving right in, doing my research, I eventually discovered the power of inbound marketing, which at the time had different names (demand generation, content marketing). The more I really looking into it, I concluded, "this is for us."

Inbound Marketing

The opposite of outbound marketing, which relies on traditional advertising and cold calling, this was a marketing strategy whereby providing valuable information and content you could attract the attention of prospects and get found by customers. It made sense to me. If we could share our expertise and be seen as the thought leader that we in fact were, maybe we wouldn't have to chase people down. Maybe people would come to us.

This revelation came to me three years ago and the first thing I did was start a company blog. In the beginning it was difficult, suffice to say I made a lot of mistakes! I didn't know what I didn't know. Looking up a very steep learning curve, I ended up, on top of all my other responsibilities, spending a lot of time, mostly between ten at night and two in the morning, figuring things out by trial and error. I'll share many of my mistakes and those made by most people in Chapter 13.

Slowly tending it over time with love, care, and lots of blog posts, I grew the thing. What started as a blog getting 40 to 50 visits a month, generating maybe one or two leads, would grow in three years to an average of 50,000 monthly visits, generating over 200 leads a month. As validation for my efforts, after all recognition is the name of the game, our blog has been named one of the top sales blogs on many annual lists and surveys. So what does this really mean?

The Numbers Tell The Real Story

We took a 30-plus consulting company that had seen flat to declining revenue and, as a result of our marketing and sales effort, moved back into positive growth mode.

In fact, we have seen top-line revenue increase from 2011 to 2014 by 17% and new business development increase 45% for the same time period. Of our new customers, more than half came from outside our traditional core vertical. And when it comes to ROI, keep in mind that we accomplished all these results without an outside sales team—there was no cold calling involved and no traditional outbound effort. By all indications, it appeared that we were really accomplishing all the things we set out to accomplish three years ago when we crafted that initiative and held that meeting where I so impulsively raised my hand.

The Birth Of LeadG2

Meanwhile, the real cherry on top of this sundae is arguably the greatest intangible—enhanced reputation and, along with it, market perception. With our blog's success we started getting requests to write articles in major business magazines. I'm asked to speak at trade functions, all of which continue to strengthen our position as thought leaders.

Our thought leader status generates more interest, turning fish into keepers, moving new customers along the sales funnel, right down to the bottom line—ROI. Our theory turned to process, which led to results. The numbers don't lie and this experience, beginning with my first blog entry, became the genesis for LeadG2. In short, if we can do it so can you.

What Is LeadG2?

I've told you a little about where we've been, in the next chapter I'll tell you where we're going and just what's in it for you. LeadG2 is a sales performance and inbound marketing company that happens to know a lot about sales and marketing. Between us, our team has over 485 years of combined sales expertise, which sets us apart from any other inbound marketing agency. Unlike our peers who specialize in one thing, be it search engine optimization (SEO), colorful landing pages, or social media campaigns, LeadG2 takes a much more integrative approach. We are not denying the importance of any of those components—in fact, we champion all of these. They are essential.

What we do differently is focus on inbound marketing, not just as a way to increase online visibility, but as a method to identify prospects searching for information related to your product or service, in turn generating intelligent leads that ultimately convert to sales and increased profits. I'll say it again—ROI. That is how we measure our success.

And just how well is LeadG2 doing? Since its inception, it has grown 100% in both of the last two years and is expected to continue this exceptional growth trend through 2015 and beyond. This performance can be attributed to the plan we put in place when we started, the same plan and strategy discussed in this book.

Your Next Steps:

- Define your fish
    - What does it look like?
    - Where does it eat?
- Define your bait
    - What will attract your fish?
- Download a worksheet from http://bit.ly/leadg2thebook

2. Is This Book Right For Me?

"You have to be burning with an idea, or a problem, or a wrong that you want to right. If you're not passionate enough from the start, you'll never stick it out."

–Steve Jobs

Who Should Read This Book?

Without getting into the nitty-gritty of titles or job descriptions, let me answer in broad strokes: this book is for anyone at a company concerned with growing revenue and improving ROI. If growth and/or efficiency are of any concern, whether you're an Owner, CEO, or both; Executive VP of Sales or CMO; VP of Marketing or Chief Sales Officer; or aspiring to any of these positions, I encourage you to keep reading.

Smarketing

We're in a new era where the lines between sales and marketing are continuously blurring. The purview and responsibilities of a marketing professional have extended way beyond traditional channel messaging, winning creative awards, having enough impressions, and the cost per thousand impressions (CPM) that you were able to achieve. Nowadays the work of a marketer is judged on driving sales, driving lead conversions, allowing the sales staff to go on more qualified calls, and ultimately driving top-line revenue and ROI. With respect to your company, if you consider any one of these variables and ask, "how can we do better?" this book is for you. Call it a marketing book for the sales manager or a sales manual for a marketing executive, whatever side you're on your end goals should be the same.

Self-Examination

Take a good long look at your organization and play doctor for a moment. How would you assess the health of your Sales Department? If it's somehow lagging, what would you prescribe to give it that shot in the arm? Conventional wisdom has always been to hire more salespeople and let them go to work. The sales force has long been entrusted to go out there and, by the powers of positive thinking and good salesmanship, make it rain. However, the game has changed and, without building in the right efficiencies at the various stages of the sales process, we'll quickly learn that this approach is not only inefficient, but potentially a big waste of money.

But let's assume you have the right number of salespeople and they're all just rarin' to go. Are they going on enough appointments? If they're not going on enough appointments, it's likely not because they're slackers; they may well be the best in the field. At the very least, there's nothing a salesperson would rather do than go on more appointments. But they need leads. Good leads. Better leads. Chances are they don't have the quality leads they need, and to ask a top-level highly paid salesperson to sit around and make cold calls for a few hours a week is not the best use of his or her time, or the company's resources. In short, it's not a realistic approach.

The focus should *not* be on getting more salespeople, but on getting your current salespeople out in front of more quality leads— *prospects* not *suspects*. That is a better place for you (owner, CEO, manager) to be spending your time and energy.

Simple Math

Let's say you have 10 salespeople and each one has 2.5 quality appointments per week. We'll define a quality appointment as one that was set in advance, with a specific agenda, and the primary purpose of the appointment is to do a needs-analysis or present an idea or solution.

As a sales organization you would have 25 new opportunities in play over the course of one week. Now let's say you have only seven salespeople, but they each have two quality appointments per day. We're now looking at 10 quality appointments per salesperson, per week, with 70 new opportunities in play each week. We are talking about 30% less personnel and 180% more output. This is a model for *efficiency*.

Call it a biological survival imperative that every business must strive for this type of efficiency. To remain effective and competitive, an organization cannot be wasteful, and one area of operation that is most often overlooked for efficiencies is the front end of the sales process, that is lead generation.

Not to say that inefficiencies don't exist in other areas. By breaking up the sales process into its component parts and focusing on each part individually, applying efficiencies at various stages along the way, the outcome will be a reintegrated and reinvigorated sales organization with greater revenue and stronger ROI.

This doesn't always mean wholesale changes or a complete overhaul are needed. Playing doctor again, this may warrant a more surgical approach. For example, I was recently looking at a client's entire sales operation and breaking it all down. We determined that he was inefficient, and consequently weak, in only three areas.
The areas we needed to look at were:

- Lead Flow
    - We needed to determine if there were enough leads coming in and enough new prospects
    - We also needed to know whether there was enough activity on the top or front end of the sales process

- Diagnosis

    - Were they uncovering a client's needs in order to bring back ideas and solutions?

- Activation and Renewal

    - Was their customer service process allowing them to maintain and grow sales?

Mending Fences

Regardless of the extent of the changes you need to make, if you're looking to drive revenue and make your organization more efficient, this book is going to help. I touched on the mind-melding synchronicity between sales and marketing departments but, while the lines between them are blurring, they do so mostly in theory. In practice, they remain two separate divisions and the tension and strife between them is a great drag on efficiencies. Salespeople complain about the quality of leads, preferring instead to develop their own from scratch. Talk about redundancy! The lead generators in marketing complain that the problem resides in the lousy follow-through by salespeople—they can't ever seem to close.

I have a solution herein to end this schism, bringing sales and marketing personnel back in synch and optimizing these valuable resources. It's a seven-step inbound marketing system that accesses powerful tools and analytics to improve the quality of the leads passed from marketing to sales while improving how salespeople exploit those leads, boosting their success rate and closing sales. Having been on both sides of the fence, I can say without a doubt that when sales and marketing are working together amazing efficiencies and bottom-line results can and will be achieved.

What Questions Will This Book Answer?

You've read this far, so inbound marketing has, hopefully, piqued your interest, but your time is money and you may be asking yourself, "What am I really getting from reading this book?" So let me tell you what's in it for you if you stick with me.

How Do I Get ROI?

All this talk about efficiency, but what does it really mean? I'll show you six ways to get ROI out of inbound marketing and how to measure them.

1. Breaking from conventional modes of thinking—to be an effective competitor is less about maximizing resources, i.e. adding new salespeople, and more about optimizing what you already have.
2. Improving your online visibility and brand recognition
3. Establishing yourself as a thought leader
4. Knowing when to close existing leads and when to re-approach dead ones
5. Losing the bloat
6. Going leaner and meaner translates to fewer salespeople with better lead intelligence, going on more qualified calls, and closing more sales.

I'll get deeper into these six ways later on, so stay with me and your bottom line will thank you.

How Do I Set Up a System to Attract More Leads?

I'm going to tell you how to make this inbound marketing system and all its efficiencies work for you and your organization. Back to fishing, how to bait the water with quality content and cast a shorter, more controlled net so those few desirable prospects, keepers who are truly interested, find you and identify themselves, rather than you chasing after them.

What Are Some Ways to Improve the Quality of My Leads?

This book is going to show you ways to provide your sales team with quality *lead intelligence,* so they not only know who to call but when to call and, most importantly in the name of *context,* what the prospect is interested in. This way, your salespeople can move their prospects along the sales process more quickly and effectively.

How Can I Get This Same Lead Intelligence with My Current Customers?

Let there be no mistake, your best customers are your competitors' best prospects. Think about this and ask yourself, how do you continue to grow and maintain revenue potential with your existing customers? Or put another way, how do you continue to bring value to them? We'll show you insightful ways to find out what they're interested in and also how to establish yourself as an expert or thought leader in their minds.

Ask a couple's therapist, continuing to keep things fresh is the key to a long-lasting marriage. The same holds true for an old customer, keeping things fresh enhances the perception of your ongoing value. Experienced managers know that customer acquisition and retention trump a quick sale. Remember, you're not transaction driven, you're in it for the long haul. Results will come.

How Do I Align Sales and Marketing to Maximize Results?

Let's flash forward, you have an inbound marketing program and you have your sales team, now how do you realize your full potential? By creating a solid partnership or *alignment* between sales and marketing is essential for your inbound marketing program to have any kind of success. One of the biggest issues getting in the way of this success is an inherent lack of transparency between the marketing and sales departments. This problem is systemic and runs deep, it will require more than just a memo or a team meeting to fix. A Service Level Agreement (SLA) between the two departments needs to be implemented so that the two teams work better together, regularly share information and feedback, collaborate on strategy, and set clear expectations and responsibilities from the get-go. Setting up an effective SLA is *not* easy, but read on and I will show you five steps to ensure that you get it right and reap all the benefits.

Your Next Steps:

- Assess how is the health of your sales department
- If it's lagging, consider what would give it the shot in the arm it needs
- Ask yourself whether you already have enough qualified leads coming through your system
- Download a worksheet from http://bit.ly/leadg2thebook

3. The Benefits of Inbound Marketing

"When you put together deep knowledge about a subject that intensely matters to you, charisma happens. You gain courage to share your passion and, when you do that, folks follow."

–Jerry Porras

How People Buy Today

No matter what the platform, whether you are B2B or B2C, prospective buyers all go through the same cycle. Various states of mind, be it awareness, consideration/evaluation, or decision/purchase, dictate corresponding actions along the way, ranging from research (what's out there?), to reading reviews (what's best?), to listing and comparing options (what are my choices?), to reading FAQs (what are others asking that I'm not?), to finally making a sales inquiry (this is what I want, how do I get it and on what terms?"). As a business you want to, read: *must*, be there for and participate in every step of this consumption process. You need to not only be relevant, but also integral. Maintaining this level of presence is mission critical.

Back in the old days, the seller had a comparative advantage in that he or she held 100% of the information needed for a buyer to make an informed decision. The salesperson had the answers to your questions with brochures, references, referrals, pricing, and so on. As the proverbial gatekeepers they controlled everything. Today, in the Internet or Information Age, this balance of power has shifted if not totally reversed. There is very little information the buyer can't access.

Think about how you buy a car these days. You used to have to go from dealership to dealership, now you just look at all the cars online. So while the sales process has not changed, remaining fixed, the point of entry is now variable. For instance, a buyer may not contact a salesperson until he or she is well past awareness and consideration, and already deep into decision mode.

Whether buying cars, insurance, or outdoor furniture; finding a doctor or hiring a consultant, buyers have already done their research. They've already read the reviews and used social media and business networks for references—it's all out there.

So Where Are You Along the Way?

As a viable business, you need to appreciate the buying process in order to know exactly how to market what you are selling. In the earliest awareness phase, your first point of contact with a prospective customer will most likely be based on expertise and reputation. If you don't have an online presence, how do people learn about you? And if you do have an online presence, how do you distinguish yourself? If you understand the buyer's journey, and establish yourself as a thought leader at every step the buyer is going to find you as if you chummed the water.

SALES FUNNEL & CONTENT PLAN

TOFU

(Top of the Funnel)
General Topics, White Papers, How-to Guides, Short Videos, Checklists, Educational Webinars, Tip Sheets

BOFU

(Bottom of the Funnel)
Free Trial, Live Demos, Brochures, Consultations, Pricing, Estimate, Coupons

WEBSITE / BLOG TRAFFIC

AWARENESS:
GENERATE LEADS

EVALUATION:
IDENTIFY PROSPECTS

PURCHASE:
CLOSE CUSTOMERS

Get Found

Blog Posts,
Press Releases,
Webpages

MOFU

(Middle of the Funnel)
More Niche or In-Depth Topics, eBooks, Case Studies, Product Samples, Subscriptions, Podcasts, Product Webinars

LEADG2
inbound · sales · results

As you can see from the diagram, wherever the buyer's point of entry, you need to be there. But simply being there is not enough; you also need to know to *how* to greet them. For example, the earliest research phase, when the buyer is first looking and exploring the great unknown, is the time when a buyer most needs an *expert*. From an initial search query your webpage, blog post, or press release could be the right hook to establish your expertise.

As we move further down the funnel from research, to looking for reviews, to checking out choices the benefits of a healthy inbound marketing plan are just as readily apparent. As buyers are increasingly time-starved and impatient, they want information when they want it—when you are open for business is no longer relevant in this process. You need to always be open and available for information purposes—24 hours a day, every day.

Understandably, everyone enters the buying experience at a different place. They don't have to come in from the very beginning. They may come to you far along in their process.

You need to be there wherever that point of entry may be. Think of it as a preemptive strike disguised as a friendly meet and greet. No matter what, it's your first point of contact and you need to be on it, delivering the goods. The more you're there along the way, the greater your presence and perception as an industry expert and thought leader, the more likely you will be considered at the bottom of the funnel and time of purchase. At the end of the day, that's where the results reside and the object here is not to get close but to close sales.

Over the course of the next several chapters, I will break this down into steps and show you exactly how to implement an *effective* inbound marketing program. But here's an overview to remind you why you've read this far, and in case you're asking yourself "what's in it for me?"

The Benefits of Inbound Marketing

The benefits of inbound marketing are many and widespread. Like most marketing tools, some can be specifically measured (e.g. increased website traffic, social media shares) while others are less tangible (e.g. developing thought leadership). All are important and beneficial to your overall marketing and sales goals. That said, here are the key benefits which I believe are going to have the greatest impact on your business:

- Inbound marketing produces lead generation.
    - In today's any-time marketplace, this is the way prospective buyers are looking, so quite simply, *you* need to be there—you need to participate.
    - With absolute certainty, inbound marketing will

generate leads and, if done correctly, it will generate *sales qualified leads*, not just names.

- Inbound marketing positions your business as a *thought leader* in your vertical, allowing you to be viewed as an *expert* by your prospects, clients, and peers.

  o Suffice to say, ours is also a marketplace of perception where reputation is everything. Think about it, no patient will leave a doctor if that doctor is considered "the best."

- Inbound marketing provides on ongoing marketing platform for *future* clients.

  o It gives you constant points of contact that will allow you opportunities to nurture all those interested, but not-yet-sales-ready prospects thereby saving you valuable time by improving sales efficiencies.

  o A good inbound marketing program keeps you constantly relevant, *in front of* your prospects even when you're not calling them.

- Inbound marketing is a great way to be a valuable *anytime resource* to your clients, especially when they can't reach you.
  - Inbound marketing puts you in front of your prospects and customers at the exact moment they need you—N*ot* when you need them.
  - Remember, your office hours are no longer a factor in the buying process. Inbound marketing allows you to be there for your clients even when you can't.
- Inbound marketing provides you with a way to gather measurable analytics and valuable information about prospects, leads, and current customers.
  - This information helps you to close new business as well as create and strengthen existing relationships.
- Inbound marketing provides you and your team with a way to *stay fresh* and out in front.
  - Showcase your expertise by writing and creating content and develop your industry knowledge by being up to date on industry trends and news.

- Inbound marketing improves your overall online presence.
  - It drives new traffic to your website, improves your SEO allowing you to be found online, and increases your connections and engagement with social media.
- Inbound marketing will improve *efficiency* and ultimately ROI by allowing your company's best salespeople to do what they do best—sell!
  - Cold calling is a waste of valuable time and a drain on the bottom line.
  - Inbound marketing is proven to be a more cost-effective and time-efficient way to generate sales qualified leads and set appointments.
  - It all comes down to ROI and, like it or not, the numbers never lie.

Your Next Steps:

- Consider what the buyer's journey looks like for your product or service?
- List the *most important* benefits of starting an inbound marketing program
- Download a worksheet from http://bit.ly/leadg2thebook

4. Inbound Brings Out Your Inner Sales Superhero

"You miss 100% of the shots you don't take."

–Wayne Gretzky

As we navigate a competitive marketplace we will quickly discover that it's a dark and monstrously unfair world out there. However, do not despair. Justice is at your fingertips. You have tools at your disposal to, not only level the playing field, but also tilt it in your favor. Blog posts, social media, LinkedIn, Google, SEO, webinars, premium content offers—the tools are all there, the question is, do you have the motivation to unleash your inner superhero?

You see, you are an *expert*—you know your market, you know your industry, you know your customers and understand their needs, you have hands-on experience, you answer the most important questions your clients ask day in and day out, you deliver results, you sell customized solutions, you have certifications and trainings, you have special interests and areas of expertise. You are, beyond a shadow of a doubt, a thought leader in your field. You are your own secret weapon!

The only thing holding you back is you. Apathy is your kryptonite and *action* is the antidote. So, lets get moving. First, to be a thought leader you have to act like one. But what does that mean?

In broad strokes, thought leaders:

- Are constantly learning and staying up-to-date on the latest industry news, trends, and best practices
- Regularly share content and resources with their network
- Participate in related conversations both on- and offline
- Readily distribute advice and tips in their area(s) of expertise
- Go above and beyond with their clients, making sure they are informed and following best practices
- Are not afraid to have an opinion, make predictions, take risks, or share their personal experiences

Emerging from the same mythology of superheroes, a *thought leader,* like his or her super counterpart, is born from darkness (or as we know it, that cold competitive expanse filled with clutter, chatter, and chaos) because we desperately need someone to light the way. Above all, we need that same someone to *connect* with. So, instead of a Batman suit or an "S" on your chest, you now have the big "E" for *Expert. W*hat are some of your new powers?

- You are now viewed as a trusted and valued resource, with the ability to build stronger relationships early on in the sales process and strengthen existing relationships by continuing to provide value.

- You now have more and better reasons to connect with prospects, partners, and clients.

- You now have the ability and opportunities to get more referral business.

- You are now sought after, getting invitations to connect and showcase your expertise (e.g. speaking engagements that can lead to new business).

- You now have the ability to control what shows up when someone Google's your name.

- You now have the ability to build your personal brand for future opportunities and career growth.

- You now have the *super power* to stand out amongst your competition.

If those are the more global end game or strategic powers, they may seem a bit lofty or big picture for our everyday needs and concerns. Down where we are, on the mean streets of Gotham City and everywhere else we do business, it's a battlefield where daily combat is fought against crime, corruption, and—most of all—our *competition*. So what are the more day-to-day tactical powers? What happens when we hear a cry for help or, even better, how can we anticipate that cry? By unleashing your thought leader expertise and awakening that inner superhero, you'll have:

- The ability to know just what your customer is interested in and when, and consequently the ability to keep putting relevant information in front of your customer right when it's needed.
- The ability to answer questions and address any objections before they are asked or presented.

- The ability to know if/when your customer has opened your email and with whom he or she is sharing your information.

- The ability to contextualize every point of contact with your customer so that you are always relevant, needed, and, above all, trusted.

- The ability to set up *more* appointments based on sales qualified leads.

In your role as a thought leader, and with a successful inbound marketing system in place, no longer will you be merely pushing a product or service. You will be addressing an important and timely need, not to mention, you will be forever spared of that dreaded "just checking in" email because your correspondence will now be sought after, welcomed, and always right on target.

So stop checking in and start sharing content. Get active using the online tools already at your disposal, be your own superhero, start saving the world and generating sales qualified leads—one blog post at a time. As an expert thought leader, staying in front of your customer and anticipating that cry for help is what's going to keep

you ahead of the competition, but what I've just described in this

chapter is like the colorful box with a "Superhero Gift Set"

inside of it—*some assembly is required*. And as you read on I will

show you step-by-step exactly how it's done. If you think I just gave

away all the secret super powers of inbound marketing, please think

again, there are many more still to be discovered.

Your Next Steps:

- Consider how you can tap into your inner sales superhero
- Ask yourself what you can do to position yourself as a thought leader
- Stop checking in and start helping—who can you help today?
- Download a worksheet from http://bit.ly/leadg2thebook

5. Seven Steps To Effective Inbound

"A journey of a thousand miles begins with a single step."

–Laozi

What does an inbound marketing system look like? So far we've been looking down at it from a highly theoretical plane, call it the macro or 747 view. We've established that it's essentially a system using online content to get sales prospects, where the prospects find you and then raise their hands becoming leads. By the gravitational pull of *Lead Intelligence*, using precise smart information and context, these leads can then be pulled or guided through the sales funnel, from research to inquiry.

Now lets bring it down a notch, say to 10,000 feet, which we will call the bird's eye view.

As we will see in this chapter, an inbound marketing system has shape, moving parts, and is an integrative daily process that is built on seven essential steps. Subsequent chapters will bring our point of view down even further to street level and even further, into the trenches, where I will walk you through each step.

I will not only show you how to implement each step, but also how to maximize your available resources (most of them already at your fingertips) and get you ready for battle. So keep reading, victory awaits!

The Seven Steps

A successful inbound marketing system must follow these seven critical steps in order to ensure the generation of new traffic from a variety of sources, the conversion of visitors to leads, and qualified leads to customers:

1. **Plan**

- Success begins with an Inbound Planning Day where you should start by

  o Assessing your current needs

- o Setting objectives and measurable goals

- o Developing an effective content strategy

- o Developing personas

- o Defining responsibilities

- o Brainstorming premium content ideas

2. Create

- Your first order of business once your website/blog is launched is to write, write, and write some more—*Content Is King*

- A variety of content will be key to your success—different types of blog posts, podcasts, webinars, video, and premium content will help you gather information about your visitors and prospects, staying relevant at every stage of the buying process from initial research to sales inquiry

- Remember, you want to be the fishing boat that works just as hard but twice as smart—chumming the water with specialized bait, attracting the most desirable and qualified prospects—getting them to come to you

3. Distribute

- Share content specifically designed to appeal to your ideal customer

- Use a content calendar to schedule strategic content distribution

- Use SEO to help you get found through keyword searches

- Use social networks like Facebook, Twitter, LinkedIn, and Google Plus to promote your posts

- Use email marketing to bring visitors back

4. Capture

- Convert visitors into leads and generate a list of qualified prospects while having the wherewithal to track their activity, interests, and buying cycle stages

- Your weapons of choice include:

  - Premium content offers

  - Compelling *calls-to-action*

  - Landing pages and contact forms

5. **Analyze.**

- Once captured, are you able to *analyze* information to meet your needs? Do you have in-depth analytics for every page and blog post? Can you set up *smart lists* and automated lead nurturing emails? Can you track your keywords?
  If the answer to any of these questions is *no*, say hello to our software partner, **HubSpot**

- HubSpot provides all the analytical tools to take your inbound marketing to the next level

- Use HubSpot to identify:

  o Top lead sources

  o Which topics/posts are read most

  o Which offers are converting readers to leads

6. **Cultivate**

- Maintain *lead nurturing* and market automation to continue to establish trust and credibility

- Marketing automation will allow your visitors to get to know you better and learn more about your company and products, while moving expediently down the sales funnel.

- Lead nurturing is vital to cultivating and building relationships with your prospects and new leads
- Lead nurturing allows you to
    - Distribute additional content while guiding them through the sales funnel
    - Provide them with more touch points and opportunities to interact
    - Stay relevant and on top of their minds
    - Automate everything to ensure no lead is left untouched

7. Convert

- Turn leads into customers by getting visitors to raise their hands and ask to be contacted
- With an inbound marketing system, you will implement both a plan of approach and conversion strategy to close new customers through the use of lifecycle stages, segmented lists, and user history

- Consequently, you are building a framework and ongoing dynamic in which your leads are comfortable, so they are no longer just cold calls instead they are *relationships*.
- Maximizing your sales efforts, optimizing the company's efficiency and ROI, you will always know when it's the right time to make contact and will have a strategic plan in place to do so.

Knowledge Is Power

Before we move on, here are some key inbound marketing terms you should know:

- BLOG
  - This is short for web log or weblog
  - A business blog will traditionally include regular entries of commentary, descriptions of events, or other material, such as photos and video
  - Note: if you are blogging for business, you should always add a call-to-action to ensure your blog is generating leads

- Call-To-Action (CTA)

  - A text link, button, image, or another type of web link that encourages a website visitor to visit a landing page and become a lead

  - Some examples of CTAs are "Subscribe Now" or "Download the Whitepaper Today"

- Keywords

  - Picking keywords is the process of determining what topics are most relevant to your target audience or buyer persona, and crafting content around those topics.

  - Identifying keywords to showcase your knowledge is how you get found in search engine results (see SEO)

- Key Performance Indicator (KPI)

  - Metrics you use to track progress toward your goals

- Landing Page

  - A webpage containing a form that is used for lead generation

- This page revolves around a marketing offer and serves to capture visitor information in exchange for the valuable offer

- Lead
  - A person that transforms from an anonymous website visitor into a known contact as part of your business sales cycle
  - This occurs when the visitor provides his or her contact information in exchange for valuable content

- Lead Nurturing Campaign (AKA: Workflow)
  - An email series triggered when someone fills out a form on your landing page or takes another action
  - These emails help guide the lead through the sales funnel, providing more content and points of contact

- Premium Content Offer
  - Content provided once a lead has filled out a landing page form

- Search Engine Optimization (SEO)

  - The process of improving the volume or quality of traffic to your website from search engines via unpaid or organic search traffic

Takeaways

- The seven steps to effective inbound marketing are:

  1. Plan
  2. Create
  3. Distribute
  4. Capture
  5. Analyze
  6. Cultivate
  7. Convert

- Download a worksheet from http://bit.ly/leadg2thebook

6. Step One: Plan

"A good plan violently executed now is better than a perfect plan executed next week."

–George Patton

Step one is the meatiest step. In fact, it's the step most people don't want to take. Lets face it, there are two types of people—planners and plungers. I would definitely classify myself as the latter. When I started out with inbound marketing, I wanted to plunge right in and create content. "Just give me the ball and let me run with it. We'll see what happens when we get there." Sound familiar? Well, this approach may work for some and, if you've got a lot of extra time for trial and error while your competitors are just idly sitting by, it may work for you. But I'd like to start out by giving you this expert tip—build a plan!

The First 45 Days

As many of us plungers can attest to, there's usually a burst of enthusiasm and excitement when we first try or take on something new, but 45 days later the thrill has diminished.

It turns out, enthusiasm and excitement are finite commodities. What we have now is 45 days worth of motion, but not necessarily in the right direction nor, for that matter, in a forward direction. Remember, the essence of efficiency is working *smart*. Working *hard* comes with the job; anyone can work hard. Enthusiasm is great, but for it to be effective it needs to be channeled into planning. A good plan will not only steer you in the right direction but will keep you focused on longer term, strategic goals. From a shorter term perspective, for all you plungers just itching to dive right in, a good plan will get you out past the first 45 days—past the itch and into a process.

Okay, so now that I've sold the Plungers on the merits of planning, where do we start? What is this process?

There are seven critical elements to a good inbound marketing plan:

1. **Define Responsibility**

    - Before starting, there are four job/functionary titles that
      will need to be delegated:

        o **Blog** or **Content Publisher**

            ▪ Someone who oversees *all* activities to ensure that
              the inbound marketing program is in place,
              operating according to plan, and remains
              consistent with the company's overarching
              strategic goals

            ▪ The content publisher makes sure that all content
              meets the company's standards

            ▪ It's more of a big picture role involving key
              publishing decisions and company intangibles
              (like branding and goodwill), <u>not</u> the day-to-day
              logistical or technical ones

- The content publisher is typically an Owner, CEO, or the General Manager of the business, they are the guardian of the corporate brand, message, and image

- **Blog** or **Content Manager**

  - He or she will be responsible for all aspects of running the content and blog for the company

  - This person must be highly organized and tech savvy

  - In addition, he or she must know how to motivate, guide, and inspire writers and other content creators to produce content

  - This person is the keeper of the editorial calendar

  - When I say tech savvy, I don't mean someone who can write computer programming code, but he or she should have a basic understanding of CMS (content management systems such as WordPress), publishing to social media, the basics of SEO, and a little bit of HTML

- This person needs to know how to load blog posts, Ebooks, PDFs—all content—on the company's web site
- **Writers**
  - Either in-house or outsourced, you'll need reliable people who can actually sit down and create the content
  - If the inbound marketing plan is the car, writers are the gas
  - Writers are essential—you can build an amazing website, devise an amazing inbound marketing plan, but without good or even competent writers it will *not* be successful and you will not get the leads you were hoping for
- **Sales Lead**
  - This person is accountable for making sure that sales qualified leads are followed up with correctly and in a timely manner

- He or she ensures relevant feedback is given to the inbound team on what seems to be working or not, so adjustments can be made on the fly

Let's be very clear here, an inbound marketing program is not about creating content for the sake of creating content or just about generating leads. Inbound marketing is about improving ROI, which ultimately means converting those leads to sales. Because ROI is so critical to your company's health, value, and bottom line, I strongly recommend that at least one dedicated sales lead be a part of your inbound team. Remember, when there is proper sales and marketing alignment, there is optimal efficiency, even synergy, and, as you will see, the results can be fantastic.

2. Target Persona

In short, *who is your target?* You need to identify your ideal customer. After sitting in dozens of inbound marketing planning meetings, you would be surprised at how many times I have seen companies guessing at who their target persona is without any data or research on their most important prospects. The better you know your prospects and customers, the better you can generate content that addresses their needs and questions.

What industry do they come from? What job positions do they hold? Are they the owners, salespeople, what level of superiority do they have? How much do they know about your product or service? Once you get through those topical questions, keep going deeper: when they enter the market to buy the product or service that you are selling, how do they do their research?

What do they typically wish they knew more about, and where do they go for information? What blogs or websites do they look at? What magazines, news, and trade papers do they read?

Other key questions to ask when developing your target persona are: What are their expectations? What sort of sales process do they expect when it comes to your product or service? What are their most common objections, frustrations?

Now as we are digging deeper and deeper, you're probably asking yourself, where am I getting all this Persona Intelligence? No spy networks or private detectives needed, it's actually more than often right at your disposal. One way is to survey your own salespeople— ask them about their current best prospects and customers. A second way is to survey your customers and ask them all the same questions. A third way is to just *ask*—this may be the most difficult way, but if you have that kind of relationship, interview your customers and get it straight from the horse's mouth. Not only is this the most direct way, but it also shows initiative and a level of customer concern and proactivity that may be well appreciated. If you take any one of these approaches, you'll get key Intelligence that will allow you to create better content and position yourself as a thought leader in your business vertical.

Whatever you do, do *not* create a target persona by guessing. It could be costly. Going back to my fishing analogy, it would be like using the wrong bait—you'll never catch the kind of fish you want.

3. Create a Blog Pledge

In many respects, this is the most important step to planning your inbound marketing program. It's certainly the most profound. In philosophical terms, the blog pledge is the existential truth about your company, the answer to the question, who are you and what is your reason for being? It's unique to your business and brand. You can call it your DNA. It defines who you are, what your blog is going to be about, and how the market and your customer will perceive you. Similar to a mission statement, it's internal, not something you share with prospects or put on your blog or website.

It's the in-house pledge that ensures everyone is collectively on the same page, in sync, working together in a unified front, and committed to and focused on the same goals.

For example, "We pledge to be more educational than promotional, we are committed to the idea that not everything has to generate a lead, not everything needs to include a download, not everything has to come with a price. To establish ourselves as a thought leader, we have to commit to teach, share, be honest, and publish all the time. Authenticity is key."

Here's another example of a pledge, "Our blog will provide useful and valuable information for current and prospective customers. We will provide information in an easy-to-read and easy-to-share format that is direct, concise, and *not* full of fluff. Our content will be honest and we're committed to becoming trusted and valued by visitors of our blog. We will position ourselves as thought leaders in our industry and will focus on providing information."

As you can see, a pledge describes a core belief and I strongly recommend that it does not have a commercial incentive—that is one sure way to repel customers. Show integrity and a higher purpose and they will come. Think Zen, the Zen rule of archery is to aim a little bit away from the target. So, go off-point to be on point. No one likes to be pitched or sold to. It's just tacky. Apply this to blogs and people will stop reading what you're writing.

As you create a blog pledge, here are some things you need to think about:

- Is there a specific *geography* you need to consider or stay focused on?
  - If you only do business in California, then part of your blog pledge should say something to the effect of "we're going to stay committed to the needs of buyers in California."
- Think about your *target audience or demographic* and build it into your pledge
  - If you have a product that appeals to moms, then in your pledge indicate that you are writing to moms
  - This ensures that you're all writing in a consistent voice and tone
- The blog pledge should incorporate what *we will do* and what *we won't do*
- The blog pledge should give a sense of your company's or brand's *personality*

- o   Do you plan to be serious as in all business, academic, and purely educational, or casual and conversational?
- o   What you don't want is a blog that's inconsistent
- To reiterate a point I made earlier, the blog pledge must describe the *core beliefs* that your company stands for

The fundamental reasons to create a blog pledge is to keep you and everyone else in your organization focused on what you need to do to ultimately drive results. It builds cohesion, unanimity, and longevity around a clear, precise message, so others can always contribute in a meaningful way.

It's an effective guidance manual so that others, from any area of the company, can write articles if asked. Finally, if you're not available, or if you leave the firm, others can seamlessly fill the gap after you're gone. The pledge outlives all.

4. Assess Current Needs

It should go without saying, but in your planning it's absolutely imperative that you write down your current needs. This step shouldn't be difficult. Probably the reason you are reading this book in the first place is because you already have an understanding of what those needs are. Identify: Why are you doing this? What are the things you are trying to address? What are the problems you're trying to solve? What is your current situation that brought you to this point? This does not need to be long, but it needs to be in the plan. Why? Because some time after that thrilling 45-day plunge into inbound marketing, in that middle phase before you start to see any success, you may need to remind yourself why you are doing this. Going back to your plan and seeing what your needs were will keep you focused and keep you on track through the long dark tunnel. Have faith in your plan— it *will* lead to results and success. Have no fear, that light at the end of the tunnel is not an oncoming train.

5. Brainstorm

Brainstorm ideas, topics, blog posts, articles, and premium content. Now we're getting to the fun stuff—the reason most of us want to just dive in and create. What are some of the exciting articles that you think your customers or prospects would enjoy reading about your business? For example, if you sell insurance and you focus on selling insurance to businesses, verses personal policies, you may want to write an article like, "10 Ways to Lower Your Company's Insurance Expenses in the Next 12 Months."

Again, you're not selling to your customers but with that Zen bow and arrow, you are staying a little bit off point to be *on point*. The key here is when you do a planning-day you need to make a long, as in *long*, list of possible articles and premium content ideas. And here's another expert tip to help you really understand how this works: Ask yourself, what is a question or objection that a prospect or customer has emailed you about within the last 24 hours? Maybe they asked, "Why are your prices 10% higher than your competitors' prices?" You have to assume that 10 others are asking the same question, so take however you would naturally respond to that question and turn the answer into a preemptive strike. Write an article, something in this vein: "What makes a product or service worth 10% more?"

6. Develop An Effective Content Strategy

When you think about your content strategy, you need to think about what type of content you want to produce. Besides articles, do you want to produce Ebooks, white papers, case studies, webinars, podcasts, videos, tutorials, slide-share, and/or newsletters? All are valuable. As part of your plan you need to decide, which ones are we going to start with? I would not recommend starting with all of them, choose just two or three types of content. Remember, as you produce content, you need to consider where it applies along the buying process and sales funnel. Is it top of the funnel, middle, or bottom? In other words, is this specific content something that would appeal to the target when they are just starting to look? At the top of the funnel, where you are just going for awareness or, at the very most, to generate a lead? Or is it middle of the funnel where content can be more niche and in-depth, as in a case study or ebook? Is this content more bottom of the funnel? Perhaps you have a download showing customers how much you charge for something. If so, you are targeting customers who are very interested in your product.

Creating great content is only half the battle. You want to be sure that the content you are publishing is being found in searches online. This is where SEO and keywords come into play. Part of an effective content strategy is to identify and list *keywords*, terms, or phrases that you want your website or blog to be associated with online. Imagine a prospect is starting to research your service, product, or industry—what kinds of questions would they ask or what words would they use in a search engine? SEO promotes the inbound flow of organic traffic to your site that, over time, will prove to be a valuable lead generation source. Remember, inbound is getting fish to come to you.

7. Set Objectives and Measurable Goals

The purpose of inbound marketing, lead intelligence, and strategies, systems, and/or programs is ultimately to generate more revenue for your business—full stop, end of story. However, you need to set goals and milestones along the way so that you know that you're on track. Think of your car's dashboard when you are driving somewhere long distance. The goal is to get from point A to point B, but you could use some helpful information along the way. Are you getting good gas mileage?

Are you cruising at the speed limit? Do you have enough oil in the car? You're not trying to measure everything, just the important things. What I would measure, especially in the beginning, are items in the following four categories:

1. Content: focus on the number of blog posts and pieces of premium content that you create in a month. In the beginning you can answer the simple question: Are you actually creating enough content?

2. Visitors and Keywords: How many visitors did you have? In how many keywords were you able to rank in the top three; in how many did you rank in the top ten?

3. Social Media: For most people reading this book, probably LinkedIn, Twitter, Facebook, and Google Plus are the core four. Do you have a presence on social media? Are you getting followers through each of those social channels?

4. Leads: Can you track the number of leads generated from all of these channels? Obviously, there is a lot more that you can track and every business is different, but you'll need to

customize in order to track and measure information relevant to you.

Here are some measures that you should all know and share with your entire team:

- **Visits**: Total number of visits to your website or blog in a given period of time
- **Visitor**: Total number of visits to your website or blog, even if people return more than once.
- **Unique Visitor**: The total number of individual, unique visitors to your site; not counting repeat visitors
- **Landing Page Conversion Rate**: The percentage of visitors to your site who take a desired action, such as filling out a lead generation form
- **Lead**: A person that transforms from an anonymous website visitor into a known contact that is now part of your business sales cycle
  - This process occurs as the visitor provides his or her information in exchange for valuable content

- **Visitor to Lead Conversion Rate**: The percentage of visitors who become leads
- **Page Rank**: Where your website or blog falls in organic search results for a specific keyword or keyword phrase

When it comes to planning, there is much to be considered. It will be beneficial if you use the inbound marketing vocabulary. Here is a list of 40 terms and phrases that you and everyone on your team need to know. I have introduced you to a few of these terms already, now here is a complete list:

- Inbound Marketing: A style of marketing that focuses on getting found by new visitors, converting traffic into leads, and analyzing performance.
  - The concept is based on marketing and sales strategist Seth Godin's idea of permission marketing
  - Marketing and sales strategist, David Meerman Scott, recommends that marketers "earn their way in" (via publishing helpful information, nurturing leads, etc.) in contrast to outbound marketing where they used to

have to "buy, beg, or bug their way in" (via paid advertisements, cold calling, etc.)

- Call-to-Action (CTA): A text link, button, image, or some type of web link that encourages a website visitor to visit a landing page and become a lead
  - Some examples of CTAs are "Subscribe Now" or "Download the Whitepaper Today"
- Blog: Short for web log/weblog
  - Blogs are usually maintained by an individual or group of people
  - A personal blog or business blog will traditionally include regular entries of commentary, descriptions of events, or other material, such as photos and video
  - If you are blogging for business you should always add a CTA to ensure your blog is generating leads.
- Blogger: A person who writes for a blog; the act of writing for the blog is blogging
  - Google also has a blogging platform called Blogspot, which is sometimes referred to as "Blogger"

- Campaign: An email marketing message or a series of messages, such as lead nurturing messages designed to accomplish an overall marketing goal

- Category: Groupings of blog post topics

  - Frequently used synonymously with tag

  - Often times a category (in terms of hierarchy) is the top-level definition and a tag may be a more specific classification beneath that

  - For example, a blog about apple pies may have a category of baking and a tag of pies

- Content Management System or Platform (CMS): A software program that allows you to add content to a website more easily

  - HubSpot, for instance, has a CMS through which you can manage your webpages, landing pages, and blog.

- Conversion Form: A form used to collect information on your site visitor

  - Conversion forms convert traffic into leads

  - Collecting contact information helps you follow up

with these leads and learn more about them

- Conversion Rate: The number of people who complete a form on a landing page divided by the total number of people who visited the page
  - You can also measure the conversion rate of an email marketing campaign or promotion, which would be the number or percentage of recipients who respond to your CTA
  - You may measure conversion in sales, phone calls, opportunities, or appointments
- Customer Relationship Management (CRM): A system that manages interactions with existing and potential customers and sales prospects.
- Feed: A data format that provides users with frequently updated content, such as a news feed
  - Content distributors syndicate a web feed, thereby allowing users to subscribe to it in an RSS reader or via email

- Hashtag: A tag used on the social network Twitter as a way to annotate a message
  - A hashtag is a word or phrase preceded by "#"
  - For example, #yourhashtag
  - Hashtags are commonly used to show that a tweet (a Twitter message) is related to an event or conference
  - Other social media platforms, such as Instagram, also use hashtags
- Header: The top part of your blog, appearing before any pages or posts
  - Headers generally include items such as logos, taglines, and navigation menus, which are meant to set the tone or theme of your blog
- Inbound Link: A link from one site into another
  - A link from another site will improve your SEO.
- Internal Link: A link from one page to another on the same website, such as from your homepage to your products page

- Each of your blog posts should contain at least one link to direct readers to past posts and related resources
- Keyword or Key Phrase: These should be used as a topic generator
  - Picking keywords is the process of determining what topics are most relevant to your target audience or buyer persona and crafting content around those topics
  - They should be used in a strictly creative sense for structural composition, reasoning, and comprehension, and should showcase your knowledge in a given field
- Key Performance Indicators (KPI): The metrics you will use to track progress toward your goals
- Landing Page: A website page containing a form that is used for lead generation

- This page revolves around a marketing offer, such as an e-Book or a webinar, and serves to capture visitor information in exchange for the valuable offer
- Lead: A person that transforms from an anonymous website visitor into a known contact part of your business sales cycle
  - This process occurs as the visitor provides his or her contact information in exchange for valuable content
- Lead Generation: The process of attracting new leads
  - A marketing tactic will drive a person to demonstrate interest in a product or service, nline this traditionally happens by providing valuable content in exchange for contact information from a website visitor
- Lead Nurturing Campaign (AKA: Workflow): An email series that can be triggered after someone fills out a form on your landing page
  - These emails help guide them through the sales funnel, providing more content and points of contact.
- Lead to Customer Rate: This is a percentage calculated by dividing the total number of customers for a given marketing

channel by the total number of leads generated in that same period of time.

- Lifecycle: A process that consists of many steps, including research, inquiry, purchase, and usage
  - Marketers need to facilitate and enrich this process in order to build healthy customer relationships
- Long-tail Keyword: An uncommon or less used keyword
  - Small businesses should consider targeting long-tail keywords
  - Generic keywords, such as "software," are more competitive than narrower keyword combinations, such as "inbound marketing software"
- Meta Description: Your meta description should be a short description of that particular page or post
  - It's a great opportunity to place some very targeted content for your audience to see on the search results page

- A good description is approximately two sentences (no more than 160 characters) using your target keywords to invite a person to visit your site
- Meta Keywords: Tags that appear in the code of a website or blog to tell Search Engines the topic of the webpage or post.
  - These have historically been the most popular and well-known element describing content of a web page
  - Search engines, however, quickly came to realize that this piece of information was often inaccurate or misleading and frequently lead to spammy sites
  - That is why search engines no longer follow this tag; however they should be used as a guide to creating a page or post appropriate to your audience
- Meta Tags: A comprehensive term that is comprised of meta titles, descriptions, and keywords
  - The tags are elements that provide information about a given web page, most often to help search engines categorize them correctly

- These are inserted into the HTML and are not directly visible to a user visiting the site
- Offer (AKA: Premium Content): The content that is provided once a lead has filled out a landing page form
  - Common examples include Ebooks, whitepapers, webinars, and kits
- Page Rank: A number from 0-10, assigned by Google, indicating how good the overall SEO is for a website or page
  - It is technically known as "Toolbar Page Rank"
  - Note: Page Rank relevancy is changing
- Page Title (or Meta Title): The page title is the phrase that shows in the blue bar at the top of your web browser when the page loads; also the bold text that shows up on a search results page when you rank in a search engine
- Permalink: An address or URL of a particular post within a blog.
- Permission-Based Marketing: A type of marketing that asks for permission from its audience and seeks to be educational

- Permission can come in the form of opting-in to receive a newsletter, subscribing to a blog, or following a company on social media
- Podcast (or non-streamed webcast): A series of digital media files, audio or video, that are released episodically and often downloaded through an RSS feed
- Post: An article within a blog
  - It can be on any topic, and it's the collection of posts that form the basis of a blog
- Qualified Lead: A contact that opted-in to receive communication from your company, became educated about your product or service, and is interested in learning more
- Search Engine Optimization (SEO): The process of improving the volume or quality of traffic to a website from search engines via unpaid or organic search traffic.
- Social Media Sharing: When web content is shared through Social Media
  - Your content should not exist in a vacuum, give people the opportunity to share your content for you

- A lot of platforms, such as HubSpot, have this built in
- There are also tools like sharethis.com or addthis.com that make content sharing easy

- Subscribe: The means through which users can opt in to receive content including email and RSS.
  - Your blog should have multiple means through which users can subscribe to your content. These should include email and RSS.

- Tag or Tagline: A word or set of words that help define what the post is about so it can be classified
  - Think of it like a filing system and these are your folder labels.

- Targeting: When you send emails to a select audience or group of individuals likely to be interested in the message
  - Targeting is very important for an email marketer because a relevant and targeted email campaign will yield a higher response rate and result in fewer unsubscribes

Your Next Steps:

Remember, enthusiasm only carries you 45 days, at the most
- Create a plan to stay motivated, ask yourself:
  - Who is your blog publisher?
  - Who is your blog manager?
  - Who will write blog posts?
  - Who will contact leads after they've filled out a form?
  - Who is your target persona?
  - What is your blog pledge?
  - What problems are you trying to solve?
- List 10 to 15 possible blog topics, start by asking:
  - What are some common questions your customers have?
  - What is your content strategy?
  - What is your keyword strategy?
  - What are your goals?
    - Weekly?
    - Monthly?
    - Annually?

- Download a worksheet from http://bit.ly/leadg2thebook

7. Step Two: Create

"We're past the age of heroes and hero kings…. Most of our lives are basically mundane and dull, and it's up to the writer to find ways to make them interesting."

–John Updike

If planning is your least favorite step this next step, where I'll cover creating content, will feel like taking that exhilarating plunge. It sure did for me. The fact that I dove off the shallow end of a half-empty pool is a different story. Live and learn! No doubt, creating content is the fun part, but it can also be a cause for panic. Even answering the questions, "What do I write?" and "How will I stand out?" might leave you feeling overwhelmed. Cyberspace can appear daunting, even overwhelming, but fear not and know with utmost certainty that you are a thought leader in your field. Remember that and you'll be fine. No matter how crowded it is online, there is always room for a distinct message and authoritative voice (*your* voice). With the right inbound marketing program in place, desirable prospects will find you and you will be rewarded.

Types of Content

Your blog and your blog posts exist to support your company's *premium content*, which is usually only available to visitors who have made their way to your landing page. Once they have filled out the required information, they are no longer anonymous and have now become a *lead*. So if your blog and blog posts are the house brand well drinks, think of your premium content as the good stuff. It's your top-shelf, top-drawer material that serves to attract leads at any stage of their buying cycle and to hold on to them as they move down the sales funnel.

Here's a list of different types of premium content offers:

- Ebooks
- Whitepapers
- Case studies
- Press releases
- Original reports
- Webinars
- Podcasts
- Videos
- Contact page
- Tutorials

- Free demonstrations
- Free trials
- Training materials
- Newsletter sign-up

If I can start with an expert tip: do *not* try to create all of them. Here is where your content publisher and manager need to identify and be in tune with your *target persona*. It may take some trial and error and fine-tuning, but find out what resonates with, and is relevant to, your customer. If you know that your customer is interested in videos or info graphics, spend time on those—at least initially— over time, you'll hone your market sense and feel for customers' needs and know when to diversify your premium content or completely pivot. There is no shortcut to mastery; it comes with experience.

Publish Or Perish

This used to be the war-cry for professors and educators: if you wanted to keep your job at the college or university, you had to write a book, get it published, and get it out there.

And do it regularly. If this sounds familiar, it's because it no longer only applies to the education sector, it applies to every business in all spheres and verticals, including yours. If you do not publish (read: create content), your customer does not know that you exist.

You Are What You Publish

I hopefully have made the importance of content abundantly clear, remember my analogy: if the inbound marketing program is your car, your content is the gas it runs on. Since it's so important, you may think that you'll just need to churn this content out. Wrong!

Creating words, putting them on a page, and doing it in quantity, is not a "strategy." Quality is the guiding light of any content strategy because you are what you publish. Your content shapes the perception of you so whatever you put out there has to be good. If it's not good, as far as your prospects and customers go, your content is clutter—that annoying stuff littering the Web, getting in the way of finding quality content, and otherwise a nuisance. Unless you are a proud spammer, you do not want to be seen as a nuisance.

Going back to our commercial fishing boat, chumming the water for those desired keepers, creating clutter instead of good content is the same as pouring fish repellent into the water—it's toxic, often irreversibly, so do not do it. When you write something lousy, you're seen as lousy, and it takes a long time for people to forget that.

Good Does Not Mean An Arm And A Leg

Creating content is a game of quality over quantity, but you may be thinking that you don't have the talent in-house to create that level of content. If you don't have the resources to do it, you may want to consider hiring freelancers or an outside agency to help you in this arena. But remember, creating good content is not synonymous with spending money. In fact, oftentimes the very best content is generated by salespeople and not by outsiders. Salespeople are your frontline; they are the ones talking to your prospects and customers, and they are doing it every day. Nobody knows how to better respond to a question that a prospect or client may have than your Salesperson.

Here are some great tactics for creating content that don't involve outside talent:

- Identify the most common questions that your salespeople are encountering and then create content around those questions.

    o This is a proactive way to address the issues and answer the questions before they are asked by future prospects.

    o If people often ask, What's the next step once a contract is signed? create a blog post that walks customers all the way through the process.

    o Respond how you'd naturally respond, if it's complex make it "dummy proof."

    o As Albert Einstein said, "if you can't explain it to a six year old, you don't understand it yourself." Take that one to heart. Your content should always clarify and never confuse.

- Identify the most common objections and build content around them.

- What reasons are prospects and customers using to say they can't do business with you?
- Identify the most common concerns of your prospects and customers.
  - What are they dealing with?

Know What You Know

These three are all great tactics, but before you even go there you must have the expertise. Expert tip: *do not* try to be a thought leader in an area where you do not have expertise. As you are establishing yourself as a thought leader, don't talk to customers about what you don't know. Stick to what you know and/or what you want to be perceived as knowing. If you are in the widget business, stick to creating content about widgets. Keep your target persona in mind, they don't want to read about pizza if they are interested in widgets. Respect and value their time, make every eyeball count, maximize the return on your effort, and remember—*work smarter*—a greater efficiency means a better ROI.

Style Points And Quality Controls

Now that you're all jazzed to start creating quality content, you may be wondering: What should the content look like? How long should my blog posts be? Other questions will come up too, like which images should I use and what's the right color for my headlines? Sorry to say, I can't answer most of those questions, but I will give you some useful guidelines. Remember, your content and customer-facing media must be distinctly and uniquely yours. It's your DNA, it's your personality, it's the way people will perceive and remember your business. Start by reexamining your blog pledge and target persona. They are your heart, soul, and vision, and will tell you a lot about how your blog and web presence should look and feel. If you know the audience you are trying to attract, this will dictate what your content looks like. To get more specific is getting too subjective, leave those details to your content manager.

Below are some simple, easy-to-follow, formatting guidelines particularly for blog posts. You can adjust and tweak these as time goes on.

- Keep each post between 400 to 800 words, an optimal range for a business-minded reader.
  - Generally speaking, most people don't have time to read anything longer unless they are interested and motivated, at which point they'll start to look for premium content and, in doing so, become leads.
- Use a five-paragraph structural format.
  - In the first paragraph, start by telling a story that relates to the issue you want to discuss in the post (ideally based around a keyword).
  - The next three paragraphs should each have their own sub-headings and detail one way in which the reader can deal with the challenge or manage the issue described in the first paragraph.
  - The fifth and final paragraph is a conclusion that ties it all together.
  - For those daunted by writing, this is actually the natural conversational format. Let's say you were telling me a story, you'd start by giving me a little

background and context, then you'd probably give me three instances or examples, and you'd finish by wrapping it up with one key thing you'd want me to remember—the take away.

Things To Remember

- Make sure you proofread and edit your work.
  - This speaks again to quality. There is nothing worse than a perfect thought expressed brilliantly with a typo in the header, or when you're trying to get prospects to take that next step—that action to move forward—and the link doesn't work.
  - Needless to say, these mishaps do happen but are inexcusably sloppy.
- Don't be in too much of a hurry to get your content out there.
  - Make sure it's right.
  - The sayings "haste makes waste" and "cut once, measure twice" have their place in the inbound marketing world as well.

- Make sure that you use an image in your blog post.
  - Internet readers are visual learners, and a post without an image is less likely to be read.
  - If you're doing a webinar, make sure that you're using images that speak to what you're talking about. Sounds obvious, but trust me!
- Headlines and titles absolutely matter.
  - Take the time to create a headline that will grab your target persona and reel them in, e.g. "Five Questions With The CEO of ___," "The Essential Guide To ___," "The How-To Checklist For ___."
- Include keywords in your posts.
  - This includes incorporating keywords into the body of your post, your title, and URL.
- Utilize keyword research.
  - This helps you show up at the top of a Google search but, maybe more importantly, it helps you identify the exact words and phrases that are being used by your

target persona to find answers and educate themselves online.

- I'll say it again—write for your target persona.
  - Value their time and intelligence, and remember to talk to them as people, so lastly: write for humans, not robots.

I will say in no uncertain terms that content is still king. According to a recent survey, content creation was said to be the most effective tactic for inbound marketing purposes, but also the most difficult to execute. Creating content that comes from a place of expertise, integrity, and authenticity does have rewards (some can be seen relatively quickly!) Research suggests that after you have published 50 or more blog posts on your website you will start to get found more by search engines. That doesn't mean that you should blast out 50 posts all at once, but if you are able to write one post three to four times a week, after 12 or 15 weeks you'll start reaping the rewards in your search engine results. I'd call that a pretty good return on your investment in a short amount a time. And that's just the beginning. Wait until those quality leads start turning into sales.

But don't pop the champagne yet, there's still plenty of work to do.

So keep it up and stay with me.

Your Next Steps:

- Decide what kind of premium content you will create:
  - eBook
  - Whitepaper
  - Case study
  - Press release
  - Original report
  - Webinar
  - Podcast
  - Video
  - Contact page
  - Tutorial
  - Free demo
  - Free trial
  - Training materials
  - Newsletter sign-up

- Consider: Where are you strongest? What do you know? What can you find out?

- Review: How many posts does it take to get found by search engines?

- Download a worksheet from http://bit.ly/leadg2thebook

8. Step Three: Distribute

"Social media is about the people. Not about your business. Provide for the people and the people will provide for you."

–Matt Goulart

Now you have built your plan and are creating quality content, but how do you get it read? If no one is reading your brilliant content, I regret to inform you that not only does your content not matter—it simply doesn't exist. You know the age-old question: "If a tree falls in a forest and no one is around to hear it, does it make a sound?" As far as inbound marketing is concerned, it does not. Hopefully, that settles that, so moving forward—How do you get the word out?

Two key guiding lights for distributing your content are:

- Publish in a way that you are found by search engines
- Publish in a way that your content is shared on social media

Content Calendar

For the sake of this discussion on distributing content, what will guide you?

It's called a content calendar and it's the map to any successful distribution strategy. Once you know what you're publishing, your content calendar is the how, when, where. In short, a content calendar forces you to think before you launch, for example identifying and evaluating all the social media networks used by your ideal customers and prospects—your target persona.

Adapt and Evolve

Are you up to speed on social media? Facebook and Twitter keep changing their rules. You need to know what's happening and incorporate it into a content calendar.

Rules, platforms, apps—the landscape—keeps changing so your distribution strategy cannot be a set-it-and-forget-it type of strategy, it has to be adaptive and altered as needed. Adapt and evolve. Stay rigid and rigor mortis sets in.

Email

Email is your steady workhorse. Take advantage of it and leverage your email database. Send content to your audience, especially those who have already expressed interest. Make sure you communicate on a regular basis—email is a great way to bring visitors back.

Promoting Your Blog

Think of your blog as a sales library where you archive the most common questions asked by customers and prospects. The most relevant, most effective, and lets just say the best blog posts will come from interactions that you (and/or your sales team) have had with clients—from the objections they have made and questions they have asked. There is no better way to promote your blog, and, in so doing, get new business than by exploiting that sales library. Depending on where your customers or prospects are in the decision/buying process or along the sales funnel, send them information that will answer any questions or objections they may have. Be proactive and be precise, do not overload their inbox— "do unto others as you would have them do unto you." A little goes a very long way. Just like quality bait, if it's relevant and welcome they will come back to you for more.

Top 10 Ways to Promote Your Blog:

1. Include the blog url and CTA in all of your employees' email footers.

2. Include the blog url on all of your employees' business cards

3. Create sponsored posts on Google, PPC, and Facebook

4. Include your blog url and a strong CTA in your traditional advertising

5. Promote your blog to your current client and partner database via email

6. Write and distribute a press release

7. Connect with local chamber of commerce and other organizations to let them know about these free resources that you're making available

   o Ask to have them link to your blog and also ask to guest post on their blog if they have one

8. Host or present at speaking engagements, seminars, and conferences

9. Promote and engage regularly on social media (don't just auto-publish)

10. Answer client questions by linking to relevant blog posts

Get Social

Social Media is here to stay and today's online marketplace is no place for introverts or wallflowers, so it's time to Get Social and join the dance.

Social Media Plan

I refer to the core four as the foundation for a social media distribution strategy: Facebook, Twitter, LinkedIn, and Google Plus, but that's not to say you should limit yourself to those. For the right content, YouTube is a phenomenal social media outlet. But if you're not making videos, it may not make sense for you. SlideShare works great for companies who are creating and embedding PowerPoint presentations. Not all social networks make sense for every company, so establish yourself and promote yourself on the networks that make the most sense for your target persona. Make sure that you are engaging in social media where your clients and prospects are online.

This is where content distribution needs a social media plan that will determine what social media platforms are right for you.

Let me say here that the creation of a Facebook page does not constitute a robust social media plan!

A social media plan is a tactical plan in support of your overall inbound marketing strategy and, going back to the bigger picture (ROI), it is ultimately there to help you capture leads and generate revenue. So what does this mean?

It means first setting some social media goals, which should be based around these basic considerations:

- Followers

- Not just followers, but followers that fit your target persona
- How many do you want?
- Activity
  - How many social media posts are you going to write per day, per week, per month?
- Sharing
  - How often will you post your own content verses content written by others?

Sharing Is Caring

When it comes to inbound marketing, sharing is caring and thought leaders must care. Sharing other people's work on your site or blog is not only good, it's a must for any social media plan, for two reasons:

- It shows that you are a thought leader, an expert in your field and not just a promoter of your own business
  - People know a sales pitch—they do not want to be pitched (especially when they are in the information

gathering or awareness stage), and will stop paying attention to you if the only content you are sharing is your own

- It allows for a reciprocal relationship
  - The people whose content you are sharing will do the same with yours
  - Sharing is a win-win situation for both parties, and do not expect anyone else to share your content if you are not sharing theirs.

Tips On Social Sharing

When connecting on LinkedIn, look for:

- People you've met or worked with (you typically don't want to connect with strangers)
  - This includes current clients, partners, big prospects, people from networking events, and past and current colleagues
  - The more you grow your personal network on LinkedIn, the more you'll be able to promote your

blog content and develop thought leadership for yourself

When following on Twitter:

- Follow any and everyone that is relevant to your topic, industry, or target persona
  - o Twitter is a medium for sharing and consuming information, as well as connecting with a variety of companies and people across the globe

When following other company pages, look for:
- Current clients, partners and local organizations like chambers, big prospects, industry thought leaders, any news sources relevant to your topics and target persona.

Old Is New

I want to emphasize that you should exploit and maximize what you already have and/or what has worked in the past; don't let it go to waste. To someone just entering the sales funnel, your old blog is not only new it's as good as gold. Expert tip: Go back into the archives and share old content. Not everything you share needs to be brand new because people don't read your content sequentially, like an episode in a television series. Unless your content is akin to *Breaking Bad* or *Boardwalk Empire,* most readers don't start with the first thing you ever wrote and then catch up.

They enter wherever they want to, and they find your content in a variety of ways, so an article you wrote a year ago may be highly relevant to them now.

You can also use your old posts and content as a best sales practice. For example, when your salesperson is talking to a customer or prospect and hears a need or challenge, the salesperson knows that a year ago you posted a piece of quality content on your blog that spoke directly to this need or challenge. The salesperson then links to the blog post (even if it was published eight months ago). That post could even be newly optimized with an updated CTA, and that is truly maximizing your resources. Do not think of your distribution strategy as a means to promote your most recent content. Distribution strategy should be based on need over new.

Social Media Plan and Social Strategy Checklist

- Identify and examine your target persona
    - Where are they most active on social media?
    - What sites do they use and in what ways?
    - What kind of material do they respond to and interact with?
- Create and/or update company pages on the core four sites
    - Is all information current?
    - Do you link to your blog?
    - Are logos and cover photos sized properly?
- Establish a growth and posting plan
    - Once your blog is officially launched, you'll want to start promoting it immediately through social media sites
    - I suggest waiting until you officially launch to really start growing your audience because every time you follow or connect with someone you are promoting your blog, so you want to be consistently publishing

new content as well as making lead generation opportunities available to these new visitors

- Facebook—Suggested Steps
  - ○ Follow other company pages
  - ○ Auto publish new blog posts
  - ○ Promote old blog posts and landing pages weekly
  - ○ Post curated content 25 to 50% of the time
  - ○ Comment on and share others' content
  - ○ Ask employees to share on their personal pages
- LinkedIn—Suggested Steps
  - ○ On your personal page, follow companies and connect with people
  - ○ Ask employees to link to official pages in their profile
  - ○ Auto publish new blog posts
  - ○ Promote old blog posts and landing pages weekly
  - ○ Post curated content 25 to 50% of the time
  - ○ Comment on and share others' content
  - ○ Ask employees to share on personal pages
  - ○ Post in relevant LinkedIn group pages

- Twitter—Suggested Steps
  - Follow other company pages
  - Follow people
  - Auto publish new blog posts
  - Manually promote new blog posts at different times of day
  - Promote old blog posts and landing pages daily
  - Post curated content 50% of the time or more
  - Comment and RT on others' content
- Google Plus—Suggested Steps
  - Follow other company pages
  - On your personal page, follow companies and connect with people
  - Auto publish new blog posts
  - Promote old blog posts and landing pages weekly
  - Post curated content 25 to 50% of the time
  - Ask employees to share on personal their pages
  - Ask employees to +1 blog posts

- Set Goals and Measure Success
  - How many followers/likes do you currently have? How many would you like to have?
  - Remember that growing the number of likes and followers is only a valuable metric if
    - brand awareness is a goal of yours and
    - it helps to increase social traffic to the blog
  - How much social traffic to your blog would you like?
  - What kind of growth would you like to see?
  - Which social media sites provide the most lead conversions and clicks?
  - How often do you want your employees to share and interact with content on their sites?

Visits Versus Leads

Remember there is a distinction, and while Facebook may get you more visits, LinkedIn may generate more leads. You will need to assess and decide where you want to allocate your resources (time and energy). I would also add that I am not in the business of getting my clients' visits. That does not improve your ROI. Traditional marketing companies may look at visits as their measure of success, but I don't and nor should you. You need to take it one step further and look at conversions: conversions to leads and conversions to customers.

Expert tip: Quality leads beat clicks and impressions 10 out of 10 times from lead generation to revenue generation, that means always! Something that CEOs and company owners will always appreciate is their bottom line. In talking to them about the seven steps of inbound marketing when it comes to distribution, I tell them that if they are present on the social media channels and if their content is so good that people will want to share it, they will achieve revenue generation. I mention this about CEOs because it seems like talking about revenue generation is when I get their undivided attention. That's when they really get it.

Distribution is in effect the full circle, going from lead generation to revenue generation, over and over again as old content becomes new again to the next customer along on the sales funnel. I don't like to rank the seven steps, but one might say that distribution is for dough, and everything else is for show. If this is done properly, with the right strategy and systems in place, your inbound marketing program will not only be a model of efficiency, it will also be an evergreen for sales. And when it comes to revenue generation, green is the color that we know and love.

Your Next Steps:

- Consider:
  - How often will you publish new content?
  - What does your content calendar look like?
  - Who will be responsible for your social media presence?
- Write down three other sources that you'd consider sharing
  - Remember, sharing other people's content is *more important* than sharing your own
  - In fact, for every social media share of your own content, you should share three other companies' material
- Find out on which social network your target persona is spending the most time
- Download a worksheet from http://bit.ly/leadg2thebook

9. Step Four: Capture

"Content builds relationships. Relationships are built on trust. Trust drives revenue."

–Andrew Davis

What do I mean by capture? As you already know, most of what you do online revolves around these two guiding principles—getting your content found and getting it shared. Altruistically speaking, you are doing this to become a valued resource to your prospects and customers. However, in so doing, these prospects and customers are taking one step closer to your business and what you have to offer. In other words, they're starting on a path to purchase as buyers and entering your sales funnel, with you as the seller. You could be meeting prospects at any stage along the way, from initial awareness to evaluation to purchase and anywhere in between. In the old days, the path to purchase was perfectly linear and much easier than it is today. Your advertising made consumers realize they needed your product, they did a little shopping, and presto they magically appeared to make a purchase. Today's path to purchase is more of a journey. So how can we steer this journey in some way to meet our prospects and customers at a mutually agreeable destination? It's called capture.

Premium Content

In today's marketplace, the capture phase is about providing premium content—information that is valuable enough to warrant an exchange of some of a customer's information. In a manner of speaking, it is information that is no longer free. In exchange for your premium content, you will learn something important about that customer or prospect to further steer him or her on their purchasing journey down your sales funnel.

This could be as simple as just a name and email address, but it could also get quite involved and sophisticated. You could ask for information about a visitor, his/her company, number of employees, type of industry, years in business, job title, and so on.
If your premium content is compelling your prospects will divulge a surprising amount of information. So now your customers or prospects have taken the next step.

You can think of it in personal terms. Let's say you are in in the early stage of courtship with a potential partner. At the moment, you're still acquaintances, but there's mutual interest. It's an auspicious start and in inbound marketing it's a capture. Nice work!

In this courtship, the prospect is saying, "I'm a little bit interested," but what they are not saying to you *yet* is "I'm ready to buy something." Now it's *game on*.

Capture Tools

When it comes to premium content, one of the first things you need to consider is what are your options—what are the tools that you have in your toolbox? Or what are the weapons in my arsenal? As you will see in the list below, they are many and they are as formidable as you can make them. In the example above, your arsenal may include flowers, hard-to-get dinner reservations, and swanky clubs, but in the inbound marketing world, you woo prospects with

- Ebooks
- White papers

- Case studies
- Press releases
- Original reports
- Webinars
- Podcasts
- Videos
- Contact page
- Free consultations
- Tutorials
- Free demonstrations
- Free trials
- Training materials
- Newsletter or weekly tip signups

These are common types of premium content but, based on your needs and your expertise, you can always improvise. The point is that premium content goes well beyond the typical blog post. It's valuable, helps drive traffic, generates leads, improves conversion rates, strengthens brand positioning, and builds loyalty. It's important enough to capture your visitors' information, via form, and to convert them to a qualified lead for further analyzing and nurturing. In short, premium content gets you closer to a sale and to the bottom line.

Guidelines for How to Be Effective

To be effective your premium content must be:

- Important
  - It has to be something for which your target persona would be willing to exchange meaningful information
  - It must be first and foremost something that your target persona is interested in
- Valuable
  - It must provide relevant information, answer questions, be credible, accurate, and altogether "expert," and ultimately worth your visitors' time
  - If your content is not valuable, you could turn visitors off and potentially lose your market credibility
- Targeted
  - It must be carefully tailored to appeal to people in the various phases of their journey and stages of the sales funnel
  - Look at the diagram below and see how different

types of premium content are effective at the different stages of the funnel

- o As you see, your content plan must be synced to your target persona at any given phase or you are basically putting out the wrong bait and attracting the wrong fish
- o I can't stress this enough—people do *not* enter the funnel at the same time—your content is not serialized, it's not sequential, it's not the first episode of the first season of *Breaking Bad*
- o You need to be able to "capture" a prospect or customer at any time

- Goal Oriented
  - Think about what your current goals are and produce content that is designed around that goal.
  - For instance, are you currently focusing on driving more traffic?
  - Are you looking to attract a new audience because you launched a new product or service? If so, do not create a white paper about last year's product
  - Your premium content must circle back to your original goals or else it's an uncoordinated effort, ineffective, and ultimately an inefficient use of your company's resources
  - Remember, the bottom line—ROI

Thought Starters

You must recognize and respect your customers' journeys and like you've heard me say before, they don't all start at the same place. One customer finds you at an awareness phase and another finds you at the evaluation or purchase phase, no matter where they are, you must be there to greet and capture them. One way to think about this is to ask, "what puts people in the market for my product?" For example, if you're an accountant, when do people need your services? Maybe after they start a new job or move to a new city. The type of premium content you might want to offer is something like, "The Ultimate Checklist to Improving Your Tax Situation After Starting a New Job." think about what's putting people in the market, and make that the thought starter from which you then design your content.

Another thought starter, depending on where your customer or prospect is in the funnel, could be, "what are the considerations people make when choosing a product?" Some major considerations might include pricing. To address that as a thought starter you may, for example, create an ebook that discusses how you charge for your goods and services. However, you may do it by writing about how people get charged in your industry—is it by retainer, hourly, flat rate?

This may seem like an oblique way to address how you charge, but it's helpful information to a prospect or customer—making you a valuable, trusted resource. Keep reeling them in and, with each new piece of premium content, they may become a sales qualified lead. You can get to the specifics of how you charge later.

How To Capture

We use the funnel to guide us by helping us create the best and most targeted content, but how do we actually lasso and corral that steer? Capturing a customer or prospect ultimately comes down to your landing page. There are a few tasks associated with each piece of premium content to ensure you are providing the best user experience, and also effectively capturing leads. First and foremost, create a landing page where a visitor downloads your offer by giving you his or her information on a form. Make this exchange as easy and frictionless as possible. If your content is very top-of-funnel, ask fewer questions because the longer the form you ask them to fill out, the less likely they are to complete it—especially if it's a first encounter.

Think of it like a blind date, "I don't know you, you don't know me; we're just getting started." Later on, when they're ready to download your pricing information, ask the tough questions.

Wherever your customers or prospects are in the sales funnel, any exchange of information should be a fair trade. If it isn't, you'll know that something is wrong. Perhaps your content is not important or valuable enough or it's not accurately targeted. Start over and once you have your premium content where it needs to be, people will readily make the exchange. A good landing page must answer each of these four questions within seconds of your visitor's arrival:

1. What exactly is being offered?
   - Be descriptive and clear
   - Give a bulleted list of what the prospect will receive in exchange for their personal data
2. What are the benefits of the offer?
   - Why is it important?
   - Explain why the visitor couldn't live without it

3. Why does the viewer need the offer now?

   o Create a sense of urgency

4. How does the user get the offer?

   o The page must always make it easy for a lead to convert.

A clunky, hard to navigate landing page is the kiss of death—it *must* be easy and obvious. There should be no mystery as to what to do when you get there and it must be dummy proof with no instructions needed. If it's not that easy it runs the risk of not working. There is a very clear and simple metric for determining how well it's working—the number of people who come to your landing page versus the number of people who fill out the form and convert, AKA the number of people that you have captured.

Quality Conversions

I look at a lot of conversion rates, some as high as 50%. Imagine how good it would be to land one out of every two fish that comes your way, and know that it's doable.

The numbers don't lie, but they can be manipulated and there are other considerations that impact this conversion rate. One is the *strength* of your CTA based on ease of the landing page, the description on the landing page, and the details that you expect someone to provide. Before you pat yourself on the back for your conversion rate, think about the quality of it. Maybe set your standards higher, challenge your team, and push to achieve more demanding metrics. We'll get further into the analytics of your inbound marketing system in the next chapter.

Software Considerations

There are many software systems out there including the one that I'm partnered with, HubSpot. Many of them take advantage of progressive profiling including a resource we call smart forms, which take into account data on an ongoing, cumulative basis. In other words, on a first visit you may get someone's name, email, and industry, on a second visit that customer will be asked for different information—you might ask the number of years they've worked at their company or, possibly, the biggest sales challenge that customer will be facing over the next 12 months, and so on. It's up to you to decide what's relevant. The essence of progressive profiling is to keep asking different questions. Smart forms are highly customizable. Questions can be mandatory or optional (do not overload a visitor with questions), and they must keep the process moving forward—guiding your customers down your sales funnel. With each subsequent visit, you will be building a customer profile, which becomes very important as you identify the best sales prospects for your company.

Expert tip: When designing a form, give a lot of thought to the information you require. Do not collect information that you do not need. It's both a waste and a potential turn-off. Also, as much as possible, use drop-down menus for answer choices instead of an open-ended answer form. There are two reasons for this—first, it's easier for the user to choose between set choices than to write on an open-ended blank form; second, it's easier to sort and process on the back end. It's virtually impossible to efficiently sort and analyze open-ended data as it goes against the software's automation process. HubSpot can do a lot of things very well, but it doesn't always know the distinction between "project manager" and "project operations manager," and it definitely can't read a long form answer to a customer's essay question. Please trust me here, use a drop-down menu!

Now that you know the criteria for effective premium content, here are some practical steps:

1. **Create a landing page and unique form:** Looks definitely matter here, include an image, a sub-heading, and social media sharing icons, but do not use the same look over and over. Keep it looking fresh and give consideration to who will be downloading it. Do not ask for information you do not need. Always keep in mind that this is where lead conversion happens, so every landing page must have a descriptive title, a description of the offer, and a unique form for access to the offer. For high impact, make it good looking, functional, and descriptively precise

2. **Include an email response on your landing page:** When someone submits the form on your landing page, they will be sent an automated email thanking them and providing a link to access the download (or instructions for next steps if it's not a download). In practical terms, what does this really mean? Imagine someone is reading your blog and at the bottom of your blog they see a CTA that appeals to them, so they click on it. Now on a landing page, they decide to download your ebook. Once they click on the download button, the very next page they want to see is that ebook. Simultaneously, what they also want with that download is an email giving them another means to access that ebook. This allows them to pick it up on their iPad, laptop, or any other device but it also allows them to easily share it. Remember your two guiding principles—to be found and get shared.

3. **Create a *Thank-You* Page:** Immediately after submitting the form your visitor will be automatically redirected to a new page on your website. While you are thanking the customer

for downloading the ebook, you are also providing a link to access the download, and, perhaps, a new CTA if applicable, like "Subscribe to our blog" or "Check out these related posts." (Think of this as cross-selling). From here they can navigate wherever they'd like on your website.

4. **Create A Call-to-Action:** Building a CTA is easier once you have built your landing page and once your forms are right. While the CTA is the first thing a customer will experience, you are creating it last so that it's completely crystallized and focused on your content, landing page, and all its related forms. One way of looking at this fourth step is like writing a news article then creating its inciting headline. In another sense, you need a product before you can create its marketing hook.

Your Next Steps:

- Consider: What will you create and promote for your first piece of premium content?
- Ask yourself:
    - What stage of the buyer's journey does it fall under?
    - What are the most important pieces of information you want to capture from leads? Ideas include:
        - Email address
        - Job title
        - Phone number
        - Company name
- Decide what kind of software you will use to keep track of your leads
- Download a worksheet from http://bit.ly/leadg2thebook

10. Step Five: Analyze

"Our greatest weakness lies in giving up. The most certain way to succeed is always to try just one more time."
                                                   –Thomas Edison

We now have the ability to analyze anything and everything and then some, but one of the biggest mistakes and colossal wastes of time is to try to do just that. Analytics for analytics' sake is interesting, but hardly useful or even productive. The goal is not to have good analytics with reams of spreadsheets and ratios. Unless wasting man-hours and having superfluous data is a goal that you have established (and if it is, we need to talk about better goals), do *not* over-analyze. So what do you want to analyze? What is truly useful information to tell you what is working, what is not, and how to adjust? What do you really need to measure to achieve your goals?

Before I give you my list, one of my major recommendations is that you first make a list of everything that you could possibly want to analyze.

Nobody knows your business better than you so, in true brainstorming fashion, take out a pen and paper and start creating a long list. There is no bad idea during the brainstorming session, so include <u>every</u> possible thing and/or activity that you'd ever want to track.

Now, look at that list and decide which metric you really want to commit to looking at on a regular basis (monthly, weekly, daily) so that you can see trends, opportunities to improve, etc. Hopefully, this will shorten your original list considerably. If not, you either seriously know what you are doing or you are building inefficiencies into your workflow, and only you know which. My advice is to err on the side of conserving time or resources.

If you are in the early stages of your inbound marketing program, the things that you will want to analyze are primarily based on *activity*. For example, these activity metrics include:

- The number of blog posts you are publishing

- The number of pieces of premium content that you are creating

- The number of visitors

- The number of targeted keywords ranking in the top three, and/or ranking on the front search page because of the content you are producing

You will also want to keep track of social media—how many followers do you have on Facebook, LinkedIn, or Twitter and ultimately the leads generated from each.

Take Note: Companies with a strong sales and marketing service level alignment (SLA) get a 20% annual revenue growth. (The definition of a *service level alignment* is an understanding, agreement, and ongoing communication between sales and marketing at an organization to help ensure consistent goals, expectations, and results). This is a very compelling statistic, but to make sure that your SLA is working you need to make sure that you are analyzing the right things. So what are they? I'll share my list with you, but keep in mind that they are in no particular order.

15 Sales and Marketing Metrics Every Organization Should Be Tracking

Sifting through the reams of spreadsheets and ratios (I've done it so you don't have to), these are the metrics that I think you should be looking at on a regular basis:

1. Visits

Whether visitors are coming directly to your website through organic search traffic, a referral from another website, social media, an email campaign, or a paid ad campaign, you need to track visits to your website and know where visitors are coming from.

2. Leads Being Generated

Track these monthly. Know the source of the lead, and not just online sources—is the lead coming from a trade show that you recently did? Maybe a speaking engagement? Individual salespeople? A print/radio/TV campaign? If a lead is coming from your website, you need to know what page on your website.

This is vital information. By attributing a number or percentage of leads to a page or article on your website (e.g. "*Services We Offer*"), you would know if there's an appetite for that information. If there is, do more to get people going to that page.

3. MQLs.

How many of those leads can you call marketing qualified leads? There's no standard definition that applies to all organizations—my MQLs are not your MQLs. That said, "marketing qualified" might mean that the lead meets the right criteria (job title, specific content downloaded, business email address, personal email address). Only you can establish that criteria—make it as inclusive or exclusive as suits you.

4. SQLs

How many of those leads can we call sales qualified leads? Again, you need to have your own definition—it could mean that someone has downloaded three pieces of premium content from you or maybe they will have just had to look at a certain page on your website (presuming you have software to automatically give you this data; if you don't, I recommend *HubSpot*). The last word on SQL is it should be so strong that it is ready to be handed off to your sales department.

Remember, the biggest frustration from business owners and sales managers is that their leads are neither strong nor qualified. Get in the habit of qualifying your leads! This will give you a clear, fact-based look at what's going on and allow you to make the necessary adjustments.

I always say, to keep a boat on course you must keep making little adjustments—this is not a set-it-and-forget-it process, it's ongoing. You can't just step away. If you do, you will veer off course and away from your goals.

5. Opportunities

How many opportunities are generated from these leads? If you have all these leads coming in and none of them are turning into real proposals, then something's wrong and it maybe a sign of a bottleneck somewhere in the process.

6. New Customers

Are those opportunities turning into new customers—how many new customer acquisitions are you getting per month?

7. Revenue

How much revenue is being generated monthly from this new business? The power of these analytics is that they break down the process into its component parts, getting us to where it matters most—the bottom line. They allow you to figure out what's going on and improve every step of the way. Analytics tell you where to focus your energies, which will make you more efficient, in turn favorably impacting your ROI. Anyone who is familiar with the theory of constraints (TOC) will know exactly what I mean. TOC is a management paradigm that views any manageable system as being limited in achieving more of its goals by a very small number of constraints.

There is always at least one constraint—bottleneck—and TOC uses a focusing process to identify the constraint and restructure the rest of the organization around it. In short, cure your bottleneck and success will follow.

8. Referral Business—Goals versus Actual

What kind of referral business are you getting? Do you plan to ask customers for referrals? Expert tip: Consider setting up a landing page dedicated only to receiving referrals. Word-of-mouth marketing is an important component to many businesses so just ask your customer, "If we are doing a good job for you, is there anyone you can refer to us?" You get the idea. Now set some goals and track your performance in this area.

9. Content Published—Number of Blog Posts

If content marketing is part of your lead generation strategy (and I strongly suggest that it be) then tracking your publishing schedule is really important. A lot of research points to the fact that the more new content you publish to your website, the more traffic and leads you will generate.

So be sure to set content frequency goals and track them. I recommend getting as specific as possible and use your content calendar to track:

- Where content is coming from (source)

- What part of the sales funnel it is written for

- Which topics are covered

- Campaigns they are associated with

This will keep you balanced and focused while identifying any areas for improvement.

10. Content Published—Premium Content

- Total

- Most Viewed

- Most Downloaded

- Landing Page Conversion Rate

- Best-Qualified Lead Source

Ask yourself a simple question, is your premium content converting readers and visitors into leads? Then do the forensics and figure out what's working and what isn't.

11. Social Media—Reach, Shares, Traffic, Leads

Every company should have a social media marketing strategy, even if that means focusing on only one medium, like LinkedIn. So tracking your overall reach (measured in followers), monthly shares (is your content being shared?), traffic to your site from social media, and the number of leads generated from individual social media accounts, are all important in knowing what is working and what isn't. Your Facebook traffic may be impressive, but are you getting more leads generated from LinkedIn? This is important to know when it comes to making adjustments. You can either spend your resources trying to convert more visitors on Facebook or you can publish more content on LinkedIn. Or do a little bit of both until you find that optimal balance. This is the art of fine-tuning.

12. Subscribers

- Number of overall subscribers to your blog and newsletters
- Average email open and click rate

Some people are going to find you and read your content, perhaps become a lead, or maybe not. Others may deem you a thought leader and like your content enough to want to receive it when you publish it—monthly, weekly, instantly (it doesn't really matter) and want to subscribe to your blog. How many newsletter or blog subscribers do you have? How big is your customer or prospect database (and are you utilizing it)? If growing these lists (AKA following) is a goal of yours, then make sure that you're tracking these metrics each month. I'd also encourage tracking your average email marketing open and click rates for these lists to identify any substantial changes—how many people are getting the email, how many people are opening it, and how many are clicking and taking the action?

13. Individual Page Statistics

What is the most read piece of blog content this month? This year? All-time? What is the most visited/read page on your website? Which single page or article has the highest lead conversion? This is done not to hand out awards, but to know what people are obviously interested in.

This will also help you shape future campaigns and develop topics that you know attract visitors and leads. Remember the two content goals I discussed—be important and be valuable.

14. Keywords

Track the number of keywords ranked in the top three and top ten or on the first search page. And you absolutely should have a strategic keyword component to your content plan in which goals are being set to continuously grow these numbers. Remember, this speaks to the two guiding principles: being found in search and shared on social media. If you're not on the front page of a search, not many people are going past the first page of search results, and consequently you not going to be found.

15. Revenue Assists

Sources, pages, posts, campaigns—an inbound marketing system is great in that it helps you attract prospects and customers you might not already know, it allows them to see you as a thought leader, and it creates opportunities for them to engage with you on their customer journey until they actually become a customer. But what about organizations with an existing sales staff? And what about customers and prospects found through traditional outbound channels or by some good old fashioned prospecting or selling technique? (Or as I call them, customers who came in the side door). In these cases, by actively engaging salespeople in your inbound marketing system, you want to use the power of inbound marketing to help pull these prospects or customers through the funnel to becoming a customer or ultimately making a sale. This is called a revenue assist. So in the real world what does that look like? Imagine you're an attorney and your meeting with a prospect, which you got through a referral from a current client. During the meeting, you learn that the prospect is dealing with a situation that involves complex legal and tax issues with having a sales force spread across various states. It just so happens that your law firm practices inbound marketing and has actually written a white paper and several blog posts on this very topic. So later that day you go back to your office and write the prospect an email with links to this content that you suspect the prospect will find important.

Having sent those, as the salesperson, through your inbound system's software and automated work flow tracking, you will now know if the prospect has opened that email, read it, and clicked on it. If so, you know that you have interest and that you are a valued resource, and using inbound marketing strategies to give you an assist with this prospect, you may quite possibly have a new customer down the line. The fact that this prospect did not come to you through a Google search does not negate the fact that inbound marketing played a role in its conversion, and what you need to measure is the monthly dollar revenue generated by any of these assists. Ultimately, the reason we're measuring is to see ROI and this assist channel could be a worthy contributor.

Analytics are important, and remember, this chapter is <u>not</u> a plug for HubSpot or any other software. You are ultimately responsible for keeping track of your own data and activity. Software is there to automate the process and to make your life a whole lot easier. I encourage you to find the software that's right for you and your organization.

ROI

How do you measure ROI? In strict quantitative terms it's profit minus your investment cost divided by the investment cost. But there is a much fuzzier math when it comes to marketing, particularly inbound marketing where some numbers have more measurable value than others.

How do you really quantify brand awareness or intent to purchase? This logic gives rise to metrics and, more importantly, metrics that matter. When setting up an inbound marketing system you need to look at your specific goals and those may not always be so readily calculable. I'm going to mention some useful practices and helpful considerations that you should take into account when measuring that almighty metric—ROI.

- When thinking about ROI it's important to set clear goals
  - Having goals is just the first part, establishing the KPI's will insure that you are on the right path to hitting *your* goals. I emphasize *your* because not all managers, companies, and/or industries share the

same KPI's. KPI's are highly subjective and relative, so make them count.

- Remember, your goal is not to just to produce content, but rather to produce content that is helpful to your prospects and client base. When done with integrity, content will ultimately convert customers. I'm only reminding you here because helpfulness by itself is not measurable.

- Implement a system to monitor and measure your KPI's with regularity

  - Regularity is essential and I recommend monthly, quarterly, and yearly, which will allow you to see trends and make adjustments when needed.

- While every business will have a unique set of goals, and with that the appropriate KPI's, there are some general activity based measures you will want to always use.

  - The following is an example of a dashboard you might want to implement and or customize as you build out your own plan.

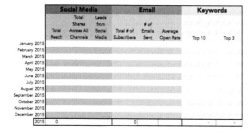

	Blog			Leads			Opportunities			New Business				Referral Business		
	# of Posts	# of Premium Content	Visits	Leads	MQLs	SQLs	Opportunities	SQL-to-Opportunity Ratio	$ from New Customers	Goal	Actual Number of New Customers	Difference	Goal	Actual	Difference
January 2015				1	1	1	10	10%	1	10	1	-90%	10	1	-90%
February 2015						1	10	10%		10	1	-90%	10	1	-90%
March 2015						1	10	10%		10	1	-90%	10	1	-90%
April 2015						1	10	10%		10	1	-90%	10	1	-90%
May 2015						1	10	10%		10	1	-90%	10	1	-90%
June 2015						1	10	10%		10	1	-90%	10	1	-90%
July 2015						1	10	10%		10	1	-90%	10	1	-90%
August 2015						1	10	10%		10	1	-90%	10	1	-90%
September 2015						1	10	10%		10	1	-90%	10	1	-90%
October 2015						1	10	10%		10	1	-90%	10	1	-90%
November 2015						1	10	10%		10	1	-90%	10	1	-90%
December 2015						1	10	10%		10	1	-90%	10	1	-90%
2015	0			1	1	1	120	1	1	10	1		10	1	-90.00%

	Social Media			Email			Keywords	
	Total Reach	Total Shares Across All Channels	Leads from Social Media	Total # of Subscribers	# of Emails Sent	Average Open Rate	Top 10	Top 3
January 2015								
February 2015								
March 2015								
April 2015								
May 2015								
June 2015								
July 2015								
August 2015								
September 2015								
October 2015								
November 2015								
December 2015								
2015	0			0			-	-

Tracking your numbers is an important first step. If your numbers aren't where you think they should be, we can help! Send an email to inboundhelp@leadg2.com, and let us know what you're working on.

LEADG2
inbound · sales · results

This example is a good starting point for building your own dashboard. Every client we work with has his or her own unique criteria but this example is what we start with and, depending on your goals and KPI's, you can expand on it. However, in some cases this dashboard might be exactly what you are looking for. If that's the case, remember that it's only useful if you monitor it with regularity and with an eye for spotting and analyzing trends. At some point, things may change and if you do find that you need help with customizing your own dashboard, my advice to you is to hire

an expert for assistance. Whatever the case, please feel free

to email me to ask for help at Inboundhelp@leadG2.com.

Your Next Steps:

- Begin tracking these 15 sales and marketing metrics :
    1. Visits
    2. Leads (and Sources)
    3. Marketing Qualified Leads
    4. Sales Qualified Leads
    5. Opportunities
    6. New customers
    7. Revenue
    8. Referral business
    9. Blog posts published
    10. Premium content pieces published
    11. Social media reach
    12. Subscribers
    13. Individual page statistics
    14. Keywords
    15. Revenue assists
- Download a worksheet from http://bit.ly/leadg2thebook

11. Step Six: Cultivate

"You can't sell anything if you can't tell anything."

–Beth Comstock

Here you are, you have some leads who have come this far because of your content. Now what's it going to take to pull them along that last phase of their buyer's journey, or down your sales funnel as you may see it, and ultimately convert them into a customer?

Before I go on, I want to stress that just because a visitor has turned into a lead, it does not mean that he/she is ready to make a purchasing decision. When someone downloads your ebook or white paper that could be where it ends—it may just be that he/she is simply interested in your ebook or whitepaper. Remember, visitors are coming to you at different phases in their own personal buying process. Some will be looking around doing general research, and others may be doing comparison shopping, looking at you as well as a competitor. Do not forget the leads that come in that are not qualified at all. They are trolling around, filling out forms for whatever reason, the least of which is to actually buy something.

Having a strategy and system to manage all leads and pull the right ones farther down the funnel becomes of paramount importance if you are in business to convert customers, make sales, and see ROI. This strategy and system is often referred to as a lead nurturing, or as I call it, cultivation.

Cultivation includes automated workflows, which are a series of emails that are sent after a lead has completed a certain action. The key to automated workflows in any lead cultivation or nurturing campaign is to determine the flow of conversation (or context) based on what action they have just taken, in other words, what they did to get them there—wherever "there" may be.

Here are some expert tips to consider for cultivation:

- Remind the lead of what action they took, e.g. what they originally downloaded
- Always be thinking about your goals by knowing where your leads are in their own paths to purchase

- Given your expertise in your industry, you should know exactly what information your leads will be looking for next and then be able to provide it
- This makes you a Thought Leader as well as relevant to your leads, hopefully making them want to do business with you
- Use a real email address, and get away from the *auto-reply@yourbusiness.com* or no-reply@yourbusiness.com
  - Not only it is a turn-off to customers but it could also be costly, especially when prospective customers want to reply and you, for no good reason, have cut off their access channel

To implement a lead cultivation system, you must have a clear sense of *what* you are sending out via your automated work flows and *when*. This is called Content Mapping. For example, Email #1 is going to look like this, Email #2 like that, and so on. Also, how often are you going to send those? Will it be every seven days? Every three days?

As it is an automated process, it all has to be mapped out, so spend the extra time to get this right because once it's in motion it will only do what you told it to do. In short, have a plan.

If you do this correctly, the benefits will far outweigh your efforts. First, it will allow you to be seen as a thought leader; second, it will help to establish your trust and credibility; third, and maybe most importantly, you are being helpful verses being pushy and creepy. Two things you do NOT want to be are pushy and creepy! This is the crux and balancing act of lead cultivation through automated workflows, you want to be helpful in guiding a lead down a purchasing path and you only want to do it in a way that's relevant and welcome. Anything else can be considered a failure. Abort. Rethink. Start over.

One of the guiding principles of lead cultivation is that all leads are *not* created equal. Based on the information that you've captured about visitors and their activity on your site—what they have looked at, what they have downloaded—you can and should customize your approach.

Part of this customized approach is called Lead Scoring or Classification. This is a system by which you can identify and qualify prospects, e.g. for a specific product, for a specific stage of the buying process, to categorize by target persona, or for an endless number of criteria so that you can further nurture or cultivate this relationship. If you've identified someone as just being in a research phase, send this; if you've identified someone as a head of sales then you should send that; or in three months, you'll send this, etc. Based on what you know about someone you can customize what you deliver next and it'd be wrong to treat any two prospects in the exact same way. Nobody likes to feel like they are just a number and this speaks to the very essence of context and contextualization.

Beyond automated workflows (emails), there are other ways to cultivate or nurture leads. First, a good thing to remember is that Marketers need to think beyond just the inbox. Needless to say, I am a big fan of email, it's a highly effective tool and great way to reach people.

However, in order to really cultivate a relationship, it doesn't end there. While we have automated workflows at our disposal, other effective ways of cultivation include:

- Social Media

- Dynamic Content and Dynamic CTA

- Sales Enablement

Social Media

Make it a habit to monitor Twitter and LinkedIn, or whatever social network is relevant to your business. Don't just post information or your own content, join the conversation! Simply posting information is way too sales-centric and can border on "creepy and pushy" territory. Get into the conversation and comment on discussions that are relevant to your business—make yours the voice of a thought leader. Also, respond to questions in a way that further validates your expertise. In time you'll be valued and counted on. This organically translates into a mode of relationship building and, when handled with care, ultimately lead cultivation.

Dynamic Content

Your website should be a dynamic experience. It should be one that leads a prospect through the funnel, from becoming marketing qualified, to sales qualified, to being a customer. Personalization is the critical component to this dynamic experience. For example, Amazon.com is probably the most successful practitioner of personalization. Simply told, my experience on Amazon is completely different from yours because my experience is relevant to me and yours is relevant to you. This is based on your history and activity, what you've recently purchased, what you last looked at, last searched for, etc. Somehow Amazon has figured out how to make it relevant and, for the most part, helpful. Keep in mind that there is a balance that you need to strike here. Just because I searched for vitamins two days ago does not mean that I want to be continuously bombarded with vitamin-related content. Over-personalization can be as bad as not personalizing at all; as with anything, moderation, good taste, and common sense apply.

Department stores and boutiques are also great practitioners of personalization. Some will go the extra mile, salespeople will send a hand-written note in advance of an upcoming sale and ask if you ran out of the last thing you purchased. The same goes for when you walk into Starbucks and they not only remember your name, but also remember your usual order. It's not only nice—it works!

What does this mean for your website? Based on which page a visitor is browsing, and on their last action, you can have a system in place whereby a note comes up that says, "Hi Steve, welcome back." This is among the many little things, call them niceties, which you should consider in cultivating online business relationships.

Dynamic Calls-To-Action

Whether on your website or at the end of a blog article, the CTAs that you use can be dynamic. In other words, if someone has downloaded a piece of content, the next time that person is on your site they do *not* need to see a CTA to download that same piece of content.

You can customize your system so that it not only recognizes the person, but also knows the next logical CTA to present. That's an example of being relevant, contextual, personalized, and most of all, helpful. It's also a light hand with a soft touch, gently guiding a prospect along their path to purchase, down your sales funnel, towards being a customer.

Sales Enablement

You can set up a notification system that alerts someone in the Sales Department when a lead is taking a certain action on your site. This would allow a Salesperson to respond appropriately. Let's say there's a prospect who is still in the research phase. He told you he'd contact you when he was ready. If your system is set up correctly, when he comes back and visits the pricing page on your site, someone in the Sales Department is instantly notified. Looking at the pricing page indicates he's more ready to talk than he was the last time you reached out. The salesperson can then contact him at an appropriate time and in an appropriate manner, focusing on being helpful (not creepy or pushy).

Advanced Targeting System

Another dimension of sales enablement is using inbound marketing tactics and strategies with an outbound sales approach. Many of you reading this book have a Sales Department that is actively looking for new business; not just relying on leads flowing in from the marketing department. Here are six steps for traditional outbound sales personnel to take advantage of an inbound way of thinking:

1. Identify your vertical

2. Do your research

    - What's new in the space?

    - Who is the typical decision maker?

    - What are their typical concerns and questions?

3. Organize relevant content based on the research from Step two

4. Create or buy a list of the companies and decision-makers that you've identified

5. Create an advanced targeted marketing campaign and workflow of five emails to be delivered over the next four weeks

- Email 1: Introduction with an invitation and offer of something TOFU (Top Of Funnel) to download.

- Email 2: Follow-up note including some research that does not require a download and an invitation to download either the same offer as the last email (if not action was taken) or something new the prospect might like (MOFU—Middle Of Funnel).

- Email 3: Include a piece of information they would be interested in right away to show that talking with you would be smart. Invite them to attend a webinar or to reach out to you for a free 30-minute consultation.

- Email 4: Invitation to the webinar with many reasons why they should attend.

- Email 5: the break up email. Let them know that you respect their time and understand that the reason they have not responded is because they must be extremely busy. You will check back with them in a few months.

Keys to Success:

- Follow up with a phone call to everyone that downloads anything in this workflow.

- Always practice being helpful rather than selling. Don't go for the close, simply be helpful!

- Thank them for the downloading and ask if you can answer any questions.

- Ask them what prompted them to take action. What will be their next step?

- Offer suggestions on what they might do now.

Other Tools

Here are some other important lead cultivation and nurturing tools that will allow you to do a better job with your automated work flows, dynamic content, and sales enablement:

- List Segmentation

Remember, all leads are not created equal. When you think about people differently (e.g. marketing vs. sales qualified, various target persona), you can optimize your workflows making them more useful and ultimately more efficient—let's not forget about efficiency and ROI.

- Lead Scoring

Understanding and putting a value on your different leads is a great practice and well worth the effort. Every company has its own calculus. For example, for target persona you may assign a certain value to a lead being a Head of Sales and another value to the number of years at that position. To identify where they are on the path to purchase, you could assign values to the pages prospects have looked at, activity, CTAs, downloads, etc. Somebody who requests a demo is a better prospect than someone who's filled out a form for a very top-of-the-funnel marketing piece. Lead scoring can help you differentiate your leads, allowing you to better cultivate and nurture. I'll keep saying it—you have to target your content to where your prospect is on his or her journey. This is a tried and true best practice and, according to the trusted research on DemandGen.com, "leads nurtured with targeted content produce an increase in sales opportunities of more than 20%." That said, you want to make sure that you don't just nurture leads at the bottom of the funnel—you want to cultivate them when they are brand new top-of-the-funnel leads, when they are marketing qualified, when they are sales qualified, when they are a sales opportunity, and even after they are your customers. This is not just about making one transaction; it's about building long-term business relationships. Remember, your best customer is your competitor's best prospect. Once they become customers the job is not over, you are still marketing to them; you're just not marketing to them as you would a lead or a prospect. The practice of nurturing and cultivating does not have a start or an end—it's ongoing.

What I call lead cultivation or nurturing is *not* crossing your fingers and hoping that something sticks. It's not mass emailing the same message to everyone and hoping that by sheer volume you get a few bites. That's spamming. Instead, you are trying to deliver the right message to the right person at the right time, with dynamic content and calls-to-action. The real magic happens when you put all of this together. What you'll see is synergy an, along with it, results. You are

no longer a transaction or sales oriented apparatus, but a

sophisticated, integrated, finely tuned machine, holistically Sales

and Marketing aligned. If this were *Star Wars*, you'd be a Jedi—

feeling and using the Force to its fullest capacity.

Your Next Steps:

- Consider: What is your plan for nurturing leads from one part of the sales funnel to the next?
- Ask yourself:
    - How you can you personalize the web surfing process for leads who are coming back to your site
    - What is your plan to separate your contacts into distinct lists?
- Download a worksheet from http://bit.ly/leadg2thebook

12. Step Seven: Convert

"You get in life what you have the courage to ask for."

–Nancy D. Solomon

Everything up to this point—planning, creating, and distributing compelling content; capturing visitors; and cultivating qualified leads—has brought you to the payoff, converting leads into customers. This is why we do inbound marketing. This is where you measure ROI, and it's where you'll look to determine whether any of this is working.

One of the things I mentioned in the last chapter is that the practice of nurturing and cultivation never ends. It's ongoing. What you do in step six will carry over into step seven and will remain part of the conversion process. Differentiation practices like lead scoring—which is making sure we're not treating every lead the same way—are critical in this final phase. Lead scoring helps determine who to follow up with and when. The goal is to always be timely, relevant, and most of all, helpful. For example, here is line of questioning you might consider as a possible talk track, "I noticed you downloaded our most recent ebook, what were you looking for help with?" As opposed to, "I noticed you downloaded our most recent ebook, now buy something." The former is so much nicer and far less aggressive. Remember, you are an expert and thought leader who is guiding *not* shoving leads down their paths to purchase. There is a fundamental difference between being helpful and pushy that you always need to observe.

Nothing changes between cultivation and conversion, but here are some other tactics that you will want to introduce and fine tune in the convert stage:

- To keep your leads engaged, get them involved in a questionnaire immediately
  - For example, ask them how they might use the product or service being considered.
  - Scenario: you sell kitchen supplies and you've already asked, "What are you looking for help with?" To which, you get this kind of response,

"We're just looking for ideas, and a proposal for how much something like this might cost." At that moment, you want to reply, "I'd be happy to help you think this through and give you some ideas on what it might cost but first I have some questions." Then you send over a questionnaire asking the following, "what do you currently have? What are your must haves and your like to haves in this new kitchen that you're contemplating?"

- o This would be an amazingly powerful next step to converting a lead to a customer because sales is not something you do *to* a prospect but something you do *with* prospect.
- o Make this your mantra and repeat it: "Sales is not something you do *to,* but something you do *with.*"

- Continue asking questions and find out:
  - o How important or critical something is. In other words, "What would this mean to your business if it were accomplished?" If it's not "mission critical" or

near the "front burner," you'd want to know this. On the other hand, if it *were* something they needed done and had the budget for, you'd *really* want to know.

- o When does your customer need this done? You must understand your customers' timetable or, in other words, their readiness to buy.

- o What are your customers' other options? You need to know this and, presuming that you have been helpful and have come to understand your customers' unique challenges, there is nothing wrong with asking this.

- o What is your customers' buying process? Understanding what they need to do on their end can be extremely useful to you and helpful to them. What's it going to take to get this bought?

- Response Time

  - o In converting leads to sales, speed is not only of the essence but may be the most critically important component.

- Depending on the industry that you are in and where the lead is in the Sales Funnel, there is an abundance of research indicating that, generally speaking, leads that are called within the first few minutes are more likely to convert to customers.
- Again, helpfulness trumps pushy, so think about how you're going to be of service prior to making a speedy response.

- Regarding "helpfulness," don't sell, help people buy.
  - Being helpful is nice, you are opening doors, but at some point you need to *close*—so help people buy a solution.
  - Focus less on selling your product and more on helping your customers get the ROI they need to perform optimally in their business, and always assume this is why they came to you in the first place.
  - In effect, help them to help themselves.

Other considerations and questions to add to your Conversion check-list include:

- Does your customer have the budget to buy your product or service?

- Are you talking to someone who has the authority to make the decision?

- Are you clear on why your customer needs to do this? What's in it for them? What is their need and what obstacle will it help them overcome?

- Do you understand their timing? Is this urgent or window-shopping?

- What are your customers' bigger goals? Do they already have a plan in place and is your product or service a piece of their plan? Or are they looking for a whole new plan?

- Again, how important or critical is this challenge?

Service Level Agreement (SLA)

Last but not least in converting leads into customers is having an

SLA in place that ensures that your company's Sales and Marketing efforts are aligned correctly. In your SLA, you should have an actionable outline of the processes of conversion specific to your company. It should include response times, talk-tracks, questionnaires, and everything I've discussed herein and more. To reacquaint you with an SLA and its purview, here is a quick primer:

- Define Roles and Responsibilities
  - Everyone should understand their role within the company, but it should also be very clear how different people and different departments could help with particular marketing and sales initiatives.
  - The more marketing helps sales and sales helps marketing, the more effective you'll be.
  - Vital here are transparency, understanding, and collaboration between the two teams.
- Lead Definitions
  - Make sure the definitions for a lead and subsequent lead scoring is clear and agreed upon by everyone

(e.g. marketing qualified lead, sales qualified lead, and an opportunity).

- This helps drive important decisions such as when a lead will be handled by marketing or sales, what questions you'll ask in a form, and whether you are actually generating qualified leads with your marketing efforts.

- Set Clear Goals and Expectations
    - When it comes to any marketing or sales initiative, you want to be sure that team goals, long-term goals, and individual goals are all clearly laid out and understood by everyone involved.
    - There is no reason that these goals should be kept secret—it's more important that everyone respects each other's role in getting to the end goal.
    - Sales goals should go beyond the obvious of normal monthly budgets—think about how often you expect them to share content with prospects or make contact with a lead, what percentage of sales qualified leads

are turned into appointments, and the kind of feedback on leads is expected so marketing can do their job.

- For marketing personnel, goals should be set for generating X number of leads each month, including marketing and sales qualified leads. They should also have goals set around number of visitors, traffic from particular sources, number of keywords you're ranking for, and how much content is published and promoted each month.

- Have a Clear Lead Follow-Up Process Outlined
  - Everyone should be on the same page when it comes to the process that will be followed when leads come through the website (or any other form of lead generation).
  - Even for those that aren't directly in the process, it's important to communicate how leads are being qualified, tracked, and followed up with to ensure consistency.

- This, again, goes back to transparency and to being very clear about who is responsible for what part of the process. It also will prevent mistakes, miscommunication, or any leads falling through the cracks because someone wrongly thought someone else was handling them.

- Automate Steps of the Sales Process
  - If you are using any type of marketing software, then you should have capabilities to automate parts of your sales process.
  - Maybe you want to set up a workflow of automated emails to go to top-of-the-funnel leads or maybe lead scoring would keep your marketing team from spending too much time going through every single lead.
  - The more time you can save your team members in the long run, the more successful they'll be in closing in new business.

Your Next Steps:

- Remember, sales is not something you do *to*, sales is something you do *with*.
- Ask the following questions:
  - How important is this?
  - Do they have the budget for this?
  - When do they need it?
  - What are their other options?
  - What's their buying process?
- Don't sell. Help people buy.
- Establish a sales and marketing SLA to determine how marketing can help sales, and how sales can help marketing.
- Download a worksheet from http://bit.ly/leadg2thebook

13. A Case Study and Some Examples of What Might Go Wrong

"If you spend your life trying to be good at everything, you will never be great at anything."

–Tom Rath

My expertise in inbound marketing is built on experience. I didn't invent it, I adopted the idea and basics of what was then called content marketing and just went for it and learned along the way. As I discussed in the first chapter, there was a lot of trial and error (underscore error), much of which I'm hoping to spare you by writing this book. That said, there's no substitute to getting your team together, rolling up your sleeves, saying "let's do this," and committing to it. Start there, take it a step at time, and you will see results. They won't come overnight but stick to it and the results (and by "results" I mean ROI) will come, I guarantee it.

Inbound marketing is not a theory, but a practice and I've seen it work over and over again. In this chapter, I'll share some success stories to help inspire you to make that first move. I'll also give you my list of possible things that can go wrong.

Going back to our fishing boat, think of this list as those little markings on a marine map, each one indicating a reef or shoal where your ship can run into trouble. Now that you have caught your boatload of quality fish, my wish is for you to get them to market and to make money. In the end, the only satisfaction I get from doing what I do is by seeing you succeed.

Before I get to things that could possibly go wrong and run your fishing boat aground, here are three case studies where inbound marketing made things go very right.

Hiregy Staffing Agency

Hiregy is a Tampa-based staffing and recruitment agency. When they teamed up with us they already had a website and blog, but were looking for that strategic partner to help them take it to the next level, and start generating real results.

The Problem:

Hiregy already understood how inbound marketing could help them develop thought leadership and provide those much-needed leads.

However, they just weren't seeing the results they wanted with their current inbound marketing efforts. Their visitors and page views were high, but lead conversion wasn't where they wanted it to be.

The Process:

The first 30 days consisted of a thorough ROI Analysis to determine what type of results were needed to achieve success, and an in-depth analysis of their current inbound marketing program.

We helped them discover their primary and secondary target personas, reviewed and optimized their existing keyword strategy, created a blog pledge, established blog roles and responsibilities, and got a jumpstart on developing a long list of blog post and premium content ideas.

The Plan:

Over the next 30 days, the Hiregy team worked hard at quickly creating new posts and premium content to ensure that a funnel of content was available and ready for publication in time for the launch. With our help, they were able to quickly facilitate the design of the new blog, import and optimize their old blog posts, create new landing pages and contact forms with the HubSpot software for more in-depth tracking, and prepare their website for the launch of their new blog. A social strategy was also put into place to help promote the blog and extend their reach to current and potential customers.

The Performance:

The most successful aspect of Hiregy's quick-start story was their ability to fully launch their new blog in less than 30 days. The Hiregy team experienced some early successes by engaging current clients with their new premium content and expanding their reach by tapping into their current database to extend their inbound marketing efforts.

Components:

- **People:** This quick launch was mostly due to the dedicated Hiregy blog staff jumping right in from day-one to produce quality content, including a brand new piece of premium content. The Hiregy team actively participated in the inbound marketing process from the very beginning.

- **HubSpot:** The Hiregy team has seen success especially from utilizing the HubSpot CMS platform to communicate their message with current, past, and potential clients already in their internal database. This has not only helped them develop a stronger identity as a thought leader in their industry, but it has also lead to better tracking and analytics for improved sales efforts.

- **Lead Cultivation:** In one instance Shaun Androff, Hiregy's VP of Client Relations, promoted a new piece of premium content through some simple email marketing. By tapping into their already established communication rapport with their database of clients and prospects it only took a simple email, sent out to about 550 contacts, to generate over 160 downloads almost immediately. While some were existing clients, it was still a valuable tool to get them interacting with the new blog and exploring their resources. Shaun shares that, "Keeping it simple and to the point, while providing highly targeted, localized content that our audience cares about is what helped with the success of this email campaign."

- **Social Media:** In a short time, Hiregy has seen a rise in traffic from sources across the board, especially social media. By using the HubSpot social media posting tools and auto-publishing options, they've increased engagement on social media and increased lead conversion overall through these efforts.

Hubbard Radio, D.C.

The Problem:

For most media companies like Hubbard Radio in Washington, D.C., a challenge they face is that they have two very distinct audiences they must constantly market to: the consumers of that medium (in this case radio listeners) and the B2B customers that buy advertising. Most have websites for their media outlets, individual station websites, but often don't have market specific websites for their B2B services.

In addition to needing an entirely new website and blog, Hubbard D.C. also has two very unique groups within their core B2B audience—general business on WTOP and government contracting business on WFED. This meant they needed two blogs on one website (DCMarketingPro.com and FederalMarketing—Insights.com) to reach two very different target personas that make up their B2B advertisers. This ultimately meant two different blog designs, two subscriber lists, two landing page designs, and so on.

Matt Mills, Director of Sales at WTOP and WFED, shares, "More than anything the biggest challenge is time. We have added an entirely new job to our current jobs and this new venture has been tough on time management." Lastly, when it comes to lead generation, both the WTOP and the WFED sales teams were in need of more qualified leads. Like most media companies, they didn't have a way for new prospects to interact with them beyond a cold call. And prospects really didn't have a way to find them on their own at all for that matter.

The Process:

We listened closely to what the Hubbard D.C. team needed, and then began putting a plan in place to help solve these individual problems.

For the first step in the process, we conducted an in-person Inbound Marketing Planning Day where target personas for each brand were identified, a keyword strategy was established, the blog pledge was created, blog roles and responsibilities were outlined, and the Hubbard D.C. team got a jumpstart on developing blog post and premium content ideas.

The Plan:

The next 30-90 days were devoted to implementing the blog launch plan and preparing the blogs for publication. This included:

- The development of optimized blog posts ready for the launch
- Premium content pieces, landing pages, thank-you pages, and calls-to-actions

- A social strategy implemented for promotion of the blog

- Keyword research and optimization

- All design elements in place including additional website pages

- The creation of contact and download forms

The Performance:

Less than three months after DCMarketingPro.com launched, the strategic inbound marketing plan we put in place contributed over 4,000 visits. In less than six months, it consistently generates an average of 50 leads each month.

The Take Away:

The Hubbard D.C. team was able to utilize the capabilities of HubSpot to have multiple blogs on the same user portal. Two blogs were created for the unique aesthetic of each brand. With our help, they didn't need to hire a web designer or purchase additional templates, which saved them a lot of time and money and expedited the launch of their sites.

Components:

- **Internal Buy-In:** One of the primary reasons the Hubbard D.C. team was so successful in their launch is due to the internal buy-in from their management team. Their inbound marketing team consists mostly of managers who have written the majority of their content and continue to participate in filling up their content calendar. They are also starting to see this attitude trickle down to sales personnel, who are proactively asking questions, getting involved, and writing content as well.

- **Cross-Promotion:** Hubbard DC has also experienced success in the implementation of an internal strategy to cross-promote their blog on their radio station websites including an RSS feed. This contributed to a significant amount of new traffic and leads.

- **Thought Leadership:** The power of thought leadership has begun to prove itself. Matt Mills shares:

  We never really thought of ourselves as thought leaders, but we certainly do now. We have found when you start writing about a subject you know a lot about, you realize how much you truly have to offer…. We even had a prospect call us directly to inquire about our services for digital advertising she

wanted to run. She had found us through our blog but didn't

even download anything—just chose to call instead.

Mayfield Plastics Manufacturer

The Problem:

Mayfield Plastics is a 96-year-old plastic manufacturing company

outside of Boston that specializes in thermoforming, vacuum

forming, and pressure forming.

They had been implementing some inbound marketing tactics on

their website including a blog, SEO strategy, and downloadable

whitepapers, however, their organic, social, and referral traffic was

low and they didn't have a plan in place to effectively capture and

nurture online leads. One big obstacle to their success included an

unclear content strategy that led to a deficit in blog post publishing

and, with only one in-house writer, it was difficult to get the results

they were looking for. In addition, like most B2B companies, they wanted a way to reach more potential leads and customers while also being able to effectively track their efforts.

They needed to stand out in their niche yet competitive industry.

The Process:

The first step taken by us was to conduct an in-depth strategic planning day at the plant in order to clearly define the needs of Mayfield Plastics, and get a better understanding of the current landscape. Target personas were outlined, specific goals were set, and there was a big focus on content development ideas and implementation. Here we also discussed the importance of a true lead nurturing strategy due to their lengthy selling cycle, which averages about three to six months. It was important that we also migrated the old blog over to the HubSpot content management system without missing a beat. This would require their existing, recently updated website to be skinned so that the new blog fit perfectly with their current design.

The Plan:

Mayfield Plastics' VP of Growth and Development, Harrison Greene, who also leads the inbound marketing efforts for the company, immediately got to work writing content that was introduced in our strategy session.

Meanwhile, our Inbound Marketing Team worked behind the scenes to start migrating the old blog to the new site, creating landing pages, forms, and calls-to-action for lead capturing, optimizing pages and old posts, and setting up social media accounts. In less than a month they were able to launch the new blog and begin promoting it across a variety of updated social media company pages and via email marketing campaigns.

Also, due to the lengthy sales cycle for this industry, we planned to make lead nurturing and lead scoring a huge part of our lead intelligence plan. This allowed us to stay on top of qualified leads throughout the sales cycle.

The Performance:

Within three months, Mayfield Plastics was consistently driving between 800 and 1,000 visitors a month to their blog and starting to capture highly qualified leads. Early on, email marketing was a big part of their strategy. Using their content pieces and the HubSpot software to nurture leads from a variety of sources contributed to quite a few important conversations with potential customers.

One particular lead who had originally rejected their price quote came across a blog post specifically addressing pricing questions, which is an ongoing obstacle for their target persona. The Mayfield Plastics sales team even referenced this post for addressing these concerns, and using their original content as a sales tool was critical in closing this deal. Their sales team was eventually able to secure the business totaling $32,000 in new revenue and they feel confident that there is a lot of potential for future contracts.

Harrison Greene shares, "There is no conceivable way we would have ever known about this company. No amount of prospecting, directory searching, or cold calling could have yielded this success because the company is so far off our radar that we would never have known about them."

Soon after, another lead nurtured through their inbound marketing program, and the HubSpot software, turned into a contract for over $48,000 of new revenue for the company.

The Takeaway:

The inbound marketing program contributed to $80,000 in new revenue within four months. Going out six months after their launch, approximately 50% of their current pipeline is comprised of inbound marketing leads and many other hot leads are currently in the funnel. Consequently, Mayfield Plastics has not only received a return on their investment but has also begun to profit directly from its inbound marketing program. Harrison adds, "LeadG2's Inbound Marketing Team showed us how to become the hunted, not the hunter."

Components:

- **Content Planning**: Changing the focus of their content to address the biggest questions about their business and services.

- **Lead Scoring and Nurturing**: A systematic cultivation strategy effectively managed leads in the funnel, even through a longer sales cycle.

28 Things To Do When Setting Up Your Inbound Marketing Program

I just gave you some successful inbound marketing stories. Inbound marketing takes work, but it's a great way to start achieving the results, namely ROI, that you're hoping for. Some of my clients exceed their own expectations and have some early success, but it's not always going to be smooth sailing. Unless you know what to look for, there are many obstacles out there (rocks, reefs, shoals, etc.) that can mess up your inbound marketing system and damage your ship, if not run it completely aground.

Below is my list of 28 things to look out for. Think of it as a map of ocean-going hazards once you're up and running and out there on the high seas.

1. Make sure to send emails from a real email address, not one called "*no reply.*"

2. Always follow up on the email nurturing that you are doing.

3. Make sure your links attach correctly and send visitors to the right place.

4. Create and/or track any keywords.

5. Create CTA's on pages other than the actual blog.

6. Have sufficient premium content and/or lead conversion offers.

7. Publish frequently.

8. Avoid acting too aggressive and/or sales-y with your content.

9. Make sure you understand your target persona and push content that is used or needed.

10. Publish frequently to social media and engage with followers (don't rely too heavily on auto publishing).

11. Send personalized emails to a segmented list rather than mass messages that sound like form letters.

12. Consider this a long-term endeavor—truly embrace the inbound culture.

13. Track many KPIs beyond only revenue and profits.

14. Integrate with your other marketing efforts, e.g.
    - going to a trade shows and sending people to a landing page for more information,
    - including the URL for a landing page in print ads, etc.

15. Remember to have management and/or other decisions-makers buy in for the program (both Sales and Marketing).

16. Communicate your goals and program with the rest of your Marketing and Sales teams (even those not directly involved).

17. Understand and measure the many different types of ROI that inbound marketing can generate.

18. Utilize content and lead intelligence throughout the sales process.

19. Make it a priority.

20. Make it your responsibility.

21. Remember to use smart content and treat all of your prospects the same.

22. Use lead scoring to find hidden leads.

23. Insist on great creative and website design.

24. Always ask for the right information on contact forms.

25. Always have your blog professionally proofread so that it is free of typos and poor grammar.

26. Never use unlicensed Google images for your blog and/or your site images.

27. Curate content correctly and effectively for your target persona—in all stages of your sales funnel.

28. Do not blatantly steal content from others without properly attributing authorship.

Your Next Steps:

I showed you several examples (in a variety of industries) of how inbound marketing can work. Now it's your turn:

- Make a list of things that can go right, and things that can go wrong.
- Download a worksheet from http://bit.ly/leadg2thebook

14. How To Use Your Expertise To Create Your Premium Content

"Sometimes the questions are complicated and the answers are simple."

–Dr. Seuss

Let's delve deeper into premium content, because it can be a stumbling block for many aspiring and current content managers. Lead generation is good in the big picture but, when you get right down to it, premium content is what captures and pulls a prospect down your sales funnel. It's prime bait and without it, your net comes up empty. But if you're like me, you won't know where to start and might find yourself staring at a blank wall, asking, "What do I have to say that's relevant enough to compel people to exchange information for it?" The answer is, a lot more than you think. Believe it or not, you are an eminent expert at your job and, in that regard, an industry thought leader and veritable king of your castle. What you know is valuable to many. So knowing that, where do you begin?

Best Practices Before Creating Premium Content

- Identify a need. What is it that customers are asking you for?

- Decide the format and sort of premium content that you want

  to create, consider the following:

  - Ebooks
  - White papers
  - Case studies
  - Press releases
  - Original reports
  - Webinars
  - Podcasts
  - Videos
  - Free consultations
  - Tutorials
  - Free demos
  - Free trials
  - Free Training materials

- Establish a tone. What is your communication style going to

  be? Is it formal or casual?

- Create a design and aesthetic style. Remember, looks matter!

  Give that some serious thought based on your target persona.

- Optimize keywords, making them searchable and trackable.

- Make sure that your content will be shareable, with proper

  links that all function.

- Make sure that you end all of your content with a CTA. What do you want your contact to do *after* they've read or listened to your premium content?

10 Ways To Use Your Expertise To Create Compelling Premium Content

The following are 10 "tried and true" ways that successful businesses create premium content. Keep in mind, this is not a checklist. You are not going to do all ten of these, although you may. You may do one and do it successfully which, at some point, may hopefully inspire you to move on and do something else. But it's not obligatory. If it's working for you it may not need fixing. You may also do hybrids. Once you get competent there is no end to your creativity and innovation as long as your premium content is useful, relevant, helpful, and effective in moving your prospects down your sales funnel.

1. Create a "how-to" for your industry. Let's say you're in the mortgage business, a "how-to" on selecting a house, essentially a

buying guide, would be very useful to those in your market while keeping you one step removed and never pushy, creepy, or overly transaction-minded (sales-y).

2. Host a webinar where industry leaders in your field (or an adjacent field such as, advertisers, lawmakers, regulators, and consultants) participate in a panel discussion. This is always welcome content. For example, if you're in the media business, imagine three major advertisers in your field discussing how they get results using advertising.

3. Show your expertise by sharing examples or case studies where you delivered positive results. It's a great framework to showcase your success as well as educate and be useful. When a business is looking to buy something or to rent a space, they love to see examples of how it's been used. For instance, if you run a hotel with a catering business, a prospective client would like to see how your space and services have been used—it entices and sets the wheels in motion on a path to purchase.

4. Create an "office hours" opportunity for your prospects to have direct contact with an expert or thought leader. Just like a college professor's office hours for meeting with students, you are opening yourself up for your prospects to get expert advice.

5. Conduct some type of question and answer session that is open to anyone. This could be a webinar, a Google Hangout, or it could even come from soliciting questions on your social media pages. Answer the questions people submitted, and then create a sheet of Frequently Asked Questions (FAQs) or a helpful guide or digital pamphlet. Imagine if you built what becomes known as the ultimate FAQ for your industry, it would be incredibly helpful to prospects and certainly go a long way to positioning you as an expert.

6. Create a step-by-step guide for something that you are both an expert in and that you typically help clients with. A guide could be extremely valuable to a prospect who is out there fishing. For example, a property management company might consider a

step-by-step guide on conducting a tenants' meeting. It's useful, relevant, and helpful rather than an aggressive sales tactic.

7. Create some type of practical worksheet that is downloadable and shareable. There are probably a lot of systems and worksheets you're already using internally that can be repurposed for premium content. If you're a financial planner, consider providing your target audience with a mortgage calculator or a worksheet that calculates how long you need to work before you can retire. Helpful and useful are the key factors here—no matter your vertical, there are always useful guides.

8. Do your own internal audit of your current sales and/or presentation materials. Like the worksheet examples, many of these materials may be useful and relevant if repurposed as premium content. It's up to you to determine what you can use, but I bet you're sitting on a gold mine of content. Anything with industry vision, sound research, and/or expertise—from a sales

pitch to a marketing presentation—can be turned into compelling premium content.

9. Review industry and/or trade association materials that are available to you. Much of this is comprised of well-researched, up-to-date information and data that can be repurposed into premium content. Provided that you get permission first, (and most trade associations will give it to you), this could be a great source of compelling and relevant material for prospective customers.

10. Turn interesting industry facts and data points into infographics. Everyone likes and appreciates infographics—they are clear, concise, colorful, easy to read, and easily digestible. If you are selling a product or providing a service with regional and/or demographic information, it's a great illustrative tool. Often it's just easier to *show* rather than to *tell*, so when it makes sense, take advantage of this.

Your Next Steps:

- Before creating premium content, follow this list:
  - Identify a need
  - Define the format
  - Establish a tone
  - Consider the design
  - Optimize keywords
  - Ensure that your content is shareable
  - End each piece with a call-to-action: where should the reader go next?

- Stuck for ideas? Leverage your expertise:
  - Create a how-to-guide for your industry
  - Host a webinar
  - Share case studies
  - Allow people to contact you directly
  - Create an open Q&A
  - Create a step-by-step guide
  - Create a worksheet
  - See what you already have
  - Review industry or trade materials

- Download a worksheet from http://bit.ly/leadg2thebook

15. Your Next Move

"A year from now, you'll wish you had started today."

–Karen Lamb

So here we are, congratulations are in order—you have made it to the end of this book. I've told you most of what I know about what it takes to implement a successful inbound marketing system and now it's time for you to get into gear and take some action. It's fair to say that information without execution is really just entertainment and, while I'm happy if you found this book entertaining, I hope that's not its end purpose. Personally, I could find countless things that are more entertaining than reading this book. What you have demonstrated by reading this far is commitment, which is the propulsion you need to get out of the gate. From here on out you need to develop some good business practices and, hopefully, good habits. But what do you do first? If you find yourself suddenly freezing in a momentary state of paralysis, fear not, I have some ideas for you.

1. Go back and read the whole book over again

   o That's right, read it again with a highlighter, and if you've already used a highlighter, re-read it with a different color highlighter.

   o Make notes and start thinking about it *not* as something that you are learning, but as something you are going to put into practice.

   o Now you're going from ideation to actuation to ultimate execution.

   o Only you know what is unique and appropriate for your business, your personnel, and your target persona. Only you know how to be relevant and a thought leader who can get your prospects to stand up, raise their hands, and say, "I'm interested."

2. Share the book

   o Share your copy or another copy with your colleagues in your department and in other departments.

- o Give a copy to the person(s) leading your Sales and/or Marketing team, get everyone on the same page, sharing the same knowledge base.
- o For inbound marketing to really work in a most cohesive, holistic, and synergistic way, there needs to be a wholesale buy-in. Consensus is vital here, it can't just be you going at it alone.

3. Identify where you are, as far as commitment, readiness, and your trepidations
   - o You might be interested in learning more right now or you might feel as if you have a lot of unanswered questions.
   - o You might even feel that there is more due diligence to be done before determining whether or not inbound marketing is right for you.
   - o Or you might be like me, and you want to dive in and get started now.

- Whichever group you belong to, know that all are valid. Once you have determined which one, it's time to take the appropriate next move.

4. One "next move" could be to schedule a strategy or planning day for just you
   - Before planning one for a team, you need to first know what a strategy or planning day might look like.
   - What would be discussed and in what order? Do you even have a strategic plan?
   - If not, go back, reread some chapters, and give it more thought.
   - Spend some time figuring out your needs and what kind of investment you are willing to make. And with that investment, what sort of ROI are you looking for?

5. Subscribe to my blog
   - Follow up online at LeadG2.com where new ideas about inbound marketing are published three times a week.

- You may also want to follow the HubSpot blog too.

- Find a thought leader and pay heed to what he or she is saying or, in other words, keep the learning coming. There's no beginning or end to education.

6. Do an audit on your own website

- There's a website called MarketingGrader.com, it's a great diagnostic tool for you to check and see whether your website is built and/or optimized for you to do inbound marketing and to start generating leads. It's free to use, so take advantage of it.

7. Determine if you have the manpower internally to implement your plan and accomplish your goals

- You may need to hire someone new or outsource.

- Not all of us are total do-it-yourselfers and that's okay.

Below is an illustration of some of the options regarding human resources and possible investments.

Getting Started

	Time	Money	Quality of Work
Figure it Out on Your Own	•Takes a lot of time •Full-time position (40 hours/week)	Cost of a full-time person	Product sometimes resembles a DIY project and lacks professionalism.
Use a Coach/ Consultant	•Saves a lot of time •Will keep you from making mistakes •Five to 15 hours/ week	Plan to spend $2000-2500/month	Ensures best practices and industry standards are followed
Have Someone Do it All For You	•Takes very little of your time •Less than one hour/week	Plan to spend $6000-10000/ month	Professional inbound marketing consultants do all the work

8. Start writing down the questions and objections that you hear most from customers and prospects

    ○ I've mentioned customer questions and objections before, and they are a guaranteed source for ideas.

    ○ Use them to brainstorm, set your wheels in motion, and get your inbound marketing system up and running.

9. Audit your existing sales and presentations materials

    o   Look around and repurpose what you already have if it's appropriate for your target persona.

    o   You may have enough to get started now.

10. Get every version of your brand on the appropriate social media platforms

    o   It's easy to do and a great first step to getting started.

    o   If Facebook is important, make sure you have a brand page on there.

    o   In fact, take the time to claim your brand on *every* social network.

11. Evaluate your competitive landscape

    o   Figure out what your competitors are doing and what resources they are taking advantage of.

    o   Determine who is the current thought leader among your peers and in your vertical. Who creates the buzz in your industry?

- Maybe no one is doing anything. That gives you more reason to get moving and make the greatest possible impact.
- Assess what your competition is doing and what you need to do to win.
- I'm reminded of an old adage—*When is the best time to plant a tree?* The answer is 20 years ago. The second best time is today. The moral of the story? Get out there and make your move.

12. Commit to starting

- It's no different than committing to getting yourself in shape and starting to go to the gym or quitting smoking.
- Carve out the time, make it a priority—at some point you have to make the commitment to starting anything. Remember, it takes six weeks for a new habit to stick.
- So decide who is going to do what, pick a platform, set a date, get started, don't look back, and, most importantly, don't make excuses! Just do it.

Your Next Steps

- What should you do next?
  - Read the book again
    - This time, do *all* the homework.
  - Share the book with people in your company to get everyone on the same page
  - Figure out where you are
    - Are you ready for inbound marketing? Or do you still have too many unanswered questions?
  - Schedule an inbound marketing planning day
  - Subscribe to the blog: http://leadg2.thecenterforsalesstrategy.com/subscribe
  - Audit your website using marketinggrader.com
  - Decide whether you have the resources internally for implementation or if you need to hire someone
  - Write down all the questions you're hearing from leads and prospects
  - Audit your sales materials
  - Claim your brand on all the social media channels
  - Evaluate your competition
  - Commit to starting!
- Download a worksheet from http://bit.ly/leadg2thebook

Postscript

I want to leave you with this: It was the moment when I absolutely knew that this whole lead generation, lead intelligence, inbound marketing effort was really going to help grow my business. I had been working with a highly sought after prospect for quite some time and, if you have ever been in sales, you will appreciate when I share with you that it had been one of those head-scratchers. You know the kind, where one moment it's moving really fast as though everything is going to work out just perfectly then, out of nowhere, it suddenly slows down and almost comes to a complete stop. Yes, frustrating to say the least! Part of me wanted to simply walk away but the prize was too significant and by all accounts we were a good solution for what they needed. I was at a loss. At the risk of becoming a nuisance, I couldn't call on the prospect any more so I decided to move on to other prospects and wait for the right opportunity to reengage. Then unexpectedly it happened—through a series of alerts I had set up on our website I noticed that this same prospect who had gone dormant was once again reviewing my proposal, looking at some relevant pages on my website, and had even downloaded a new piece of premium content that we'd just posted one week prior. I knew that this was my opportunity, that this was exactly the moment I'd been preparing for—not the moment when I was ready—but the moment when he'd be ready and interested. I timed my call perfectly. When he answered, before I could even say a word, he said that he'd just been talking to his colleagues about my company and some of the services we offer. He asked me when I might be available to come in for a meeting as they were now motivated and ready to make it happen. The sale closed shortly after and I give all the credit to having great lead intelligence. It's not about knowing whom to call, it's about knowing *when* to call and what to say that will interest them. Cold calling is certainly an option, but I liken cold calling to a game of chance whereas working a lead generation strategy that utilizes lead intelligence is a game of chess—both perfectly viable, one takes skill, the other takes money. You decide which one's right for you and your ROI.